★ ★ ★

THE

FRONTLINE GENERATION

D0958751

THE FRONTLINE GENERATION:

How We Served Post 9/11

MARJORIE K. EASTMAN

LONGBOW PUBLISHING

NASHVILLE, TENNESSEE

Published in Nashville, Tennessee, by Longbow Six Publishing.

All photographs are property of Marjorie K. Eastman, except where otherwise noted.

Library of Congress Cataloging-in-Publication Data
Library of Congress Control Number: 2016911420
Eastman, Marjorie K.
The frontline generation.

ISBN: 978-0-9977615-9-7 (hardcover)
ISBN: 978-0-9977615-6-6 (paperback)
ISBN: 978-0-9977615-8-0 (e-book)

Printed in the United States of America

To every person who finds a way to serve,

especially to those with whom I served,

my Frontline Generation.

And with all my love to Charles and Henk.

TABLE OF CONTENTS

Prologue
ix   *How I Met Your Mother* (C. W. EASTMAN)

Preface
xiii   *The 1 Percent We Should Be Talking About*

Introduction
xix   *Fist Full of Glitter*

Part 1: The Road to Command
1   *You Have a Choice*

7   *Passion Chase*

11   *Patriotic Guilt*

15   *Sometimes All You Should Do Is Smile*

19   *Chart Your Own Path*

25   *Collect and Wear Pearls of Wisdom*

31   *Yes Men and No Men*

35   *Arrive Before You Arrive*

Part II: In Command and Mobilization
41   *Embrace the Suck*

45   *Never Turn Down a Command*

49   *Perfect Discipline*

55   *Perpetual Optimism*

59   *Profiles in Courage*

63   *There Is No Bench Team*

TABLE OF CONTENTS

Part 3: Afghanistan

79 *You See a Light, You Don't Hear One*

89 *Sometimes You Should Cry*

97 *Christmas Lights All Year*

109 *Asking the Right Questions*

119 *Close Calls Don't Discriminate*

133 *Never Shower Alone*

143 *Easier to Ask Forgiveness Than Permission*

157 *What Color Is Your Cape?*

165 *Skin in the Game*

173 *For Love of ~~Country~~ . . . My Soldiers*

187 *Like a Girl*

Epilogue

199 *Service Is a Force that Gives us Meaning*

207 *Acknowledgments*

209 *Endnotes*

216 *About the Author*

PROLOGUE

★ ★ ★

How I Met Your Mother

C. W. EASTMAN

By the time you were born, I had spent nearly the majority of my life serving in the United States Army. I grew up in 3rd Ranger Battalion and parachuted into Afghanistan with my band of brothers on October 19, 2001. Since that jump, I have served seventeen combat deployments; years of my life have been spent in combat—on the ground and now in the air as an attack helicopter pilot. The deployment, however, that changed my life forever was in 2003 when I met your mother, Marjorie.

We were both enlisted at the time, and she had probably been in the army for about a day and became an activated reservist on day two. I could tell instantly that she had the drive, desire, and tenacity to make a difference. She was probably one of the lowest-ranking soldiers on our forward operations base near Iraq, but when she walked into a room you felt her presence. She looked you squarely in the eye, disarmed you with a smile, and would succinctly get to the point of whatever she had to say. When she spoke you knew—as your grandma fondly says of her—"Don't dare underestimate this smart cookie." She would leave you feeling good about yourself. I knew instantly I wanted to spend the rest of my life with her.

It wasn't that easy, though. Your mom was going places and was all business. We became friends and would eat meals with the same group of people, often square C rations ("c-rats," as we call them) of scrambled eggs and salsa, or perhaps an occasional *shawarma* from the local market. Like all soldiers deployed overseas, we shared stories about our families, faith, and what we hoped and dreamed for once we returned home. Your mom told me then that she planned on getting her commission and becoming an officer. I remember asking her, "You already have your college degree, why didn't you just go straight into the army as an officer?" She replied, "I want to be enlisted first so that I won't forget where it all begins and how it feels to be led." She was already on her way to becoming the number-one–ranked military intelligence company commander in Eastern Afghanistan.

I have seen many examples of leadership over the past decade, fighting in Afghanistan and Iraq. I have learned what a great leader can do for a unit, and the sacrifices that are required. As you are about to read, your mom is the kind of person whose compelling leadership convinced soldiers to extend their service obligations to continue to be a part of their company's mission even after the stop-loss policy was lifted. I recall seeing the looks in their eyes as they spoke with your mom (their commander) and I could see the look in her eyes that she genuinely cared for each of them too. I believe their decisions to stay were partly influenced because they trusted her—they trusted in her—and they knew she would take care of them through hell and back.

They had every reason to do so. From her early days as an enlisted soldier, through all those growing years as a young officer, I had the honor of watching your mom's military career, all the way up to her final deployment as a company commander in Afghanistan. By the very nature of her job as a commander, she would have relatively few people that she would be able to talk with uncensored. It can be very lonely as a leader. I wanted to be there for her but knew her ability to call or write home would be limited.

So I gave her an empty journal.

I encouraged her to write about her deployment, those tough decisions she would have to make as a commander, and to also write me letters in her journal, and I would read them when she returned home. She did just that. Every day she was deployed, she made a journal entry. Just before she would go to bed for the night, which often was for only four to six hours at a time, she captured the story of the day. Those journal entries, in addition to the stories of her road to command, are a treasure chest of lessons—and they are a part of our country's military history. Moreover, they help define our post 9/11 generation of service members.

For you, she began to compile those raw, unedited moments—so many of which are lessons that only a female veteran can share. Before I read her journal, I only got snippets of information and details of your mom's deployment through short and infrequent phone conversations while she was deployed. She was immensely proud of her soldiers—many of whom were working at several levels of responsibility above their ranks because of the trust that your mom had in them.

I could also tell she wished that she could do much more. Your mom felt as if she had the weight of the world on her shoulders, and she felt that because she cared. She was one of the few leaders I have met in my life who *earned* a soldier's admiration.

You are about to understand why senior noncommissioned officers (NCOs) cried at her change of command ceremony, and why soldiers sought out your grandparents at a Yellow Ribbon Program reunion event after they returned home. They wanted to tell them how your mom took care of them and that they would have followed her anywhere. I believe the admiration she attained is because she got it right from the very beginning of her time wearing a uniform—she always remembered it was about *service*. Service inspired her and she in turn inspired those around her. It was my good fortune that I not only served in uniform with a person like your mom, but that she became my best friend and wife.[1]

That reminds me to address one last thing, the obvious thing. Soldiers are also wives, mothers, daughters, sisters, and girlfriends. I watched your mom destroy ridiculous stereotypes. She proved that at the end of the day, a good soldier is a good soldier, and a great leader is a great leader. Gender does not qualify or disqualify you from becoming either of these.

There are gender-specific experiences that will be eye-opening for all who read them. I was shocked to read journal entries that described unbelievable and unnecessary encounters she faced because she is a woman. But they show how she, and other soldiers she served with, navigated these challenges with grit and grace, and how you might do the same in your own unique circumstance.

Little did we know your first battle in life would be at six months old . . .

PREFACE

★ ★ ★

The 1 Percent We Should Be Talking About

"The 1 percent" is commonly used to describe the wealthiest people in our society. The discussion around that term is typically about the growing wealth gap between America's elite and the rest of the country. But what if we have that all wrong? What if I were to tell you that the greatest value you could add to your life was not monetary? What if, as a nation, we should be most concerned about the service gap? During the past decade, as the military has been engaged in the longest period of sustained conflict in the nation's history, just one-half of one percent of American adults has served on active duty.[2]

And what if you were told that the most concerning aspect of this military–civilian gap is the missed opportunity? Service not only unearths purpose for one's life, but it unites and helps us become leaders.

The post 9/11 generation of service members are the 1 percent of our society that we should be talking about. They are the untapped reservoir of leaders in our communities who have been strengthened by the unique difficulties of post 9/11 service. In his recent book, *David and Goliath,* author Malcolm Gladwell posed the following question in relation to the effect of the German air offensive on the British population during World War II. I believe this question is also relevant in regards to those who served in my generation: "The right question is whether we as a society need people who have emerged from some kind of trauma—and the answer is that we plainly do . . . There are times and places when all of us depend on people who have been hardened by their experiences."[3]

I didn't immediately or fully recognize my good fortune of being a post 9/11 service member. It actually hit me like a ton of bricks on an idle Wednesday afternoon.

Nothing happens on a Wednesday, right? Except on that particular day, the doctor from Vanderbilt's Children's Hospital told my husband and me that our six-month-old baby had cancer. *Neuroblastoma* is the word the pediatric oncologist used. She told us the tumor removed from our baby's abdomen the day before had tested positive for this rare form of infant cancer. Found in approximately 800 children in the United States every year, in 2012 our son was part of that tally.[4] However, the only number that stuck was the mortality rate—it could be upwards of 70 percent.[5]

We braced for the worst and fought for the best. The fog of war from those first few days, and the grind of the months that followed as our son underwent numerous tests, scans, and needle pokes, was absolutely agonizing. As new parents, our hearts were breaking. With so many things to worry about when you're a new parent, *no parent* ever expects to worry about cancer. We were far from naïve parents, though. We were both combat veterans, and our ability to withstand hardship and pain—to survive this special kind of hell—can be largely attributed to the hardening we had already endured in our lives. Moreover, that background had prepared us to navigate the unexpected, especially the shocking, difficult, and disruptive events that are so different from what you thought would happen in your life.

It was hindsight that allowed us to understand this. In the middle of that battle, we didn't stop to reflect on the unique characteristics we both have from serving on the front lines for over a decade. It was only after our son passed the seminal milestone of one year cancer-free that we began to realize he was, indeed, a cancer survivor. That's when I knew I had to capture what helped me survive that year.

Of course, I always wanted my son to know about my time in uniform. I figured one day he would rummage through the bookshelves in our office and stumble upon the daily journals I kept of my time in combat. I planned to tell him that his mom was a soldier who deployed in support of Operation Iraqi Freedom and Operation Enduring Freedom in Afghanistan. I realized though, I especially wanted him to know about my time in uniform because of how it helped me get through his fight with cancer.

I began to write. Over a year, when my son was napping or during those long lonely nights my husband was deployed (again), I collected the lessons that changed my life—that changed me. I started to decipher the shorthand in my journal, from the entries that explained why I had to shower with my rifle hanging on the towel hook next to me, to others that were about the people I served with and how much they inspired me.[6] In fact, I thought a lot about those men and women with whom I had served. And on a long seven-hour drive to Alabama toward the end of that year, I had an epiphany.

With my now two-year-old son packed in our Jeep, I took a road trip to lower Alabama to visit my husband, who was stationed there on temporary duty. What one would have expected to be the unforgettable memory from that drive—such as witnessing the extreme velocity at which a Matchbox car can be hurled at the dash from the back seat, or breaking a record for how many times a person can possibly sing the ABC song—this all paled in comparison. A simple highway sign caught my attention and shook me to my core.

Just past the Alabama State Welcome Center, which is impossible to miss from its landmark Saturn 1B Rocket, a section of Interstate 65 is recognized as the Global War on Terror Memorial Highway. When I read the sign, I was immediately stunned. First, I thought, *wait a minute . . . we still have troops overseas fighting this war. Hell, we still have a tired and seasoned intelligence and law enforcement community here at home, fighting this war*. A sign felt like someone had declared it over, done, mission accomplished.[7]

What bothered me most about that sign, however, was this: the emphasis of the memorial was on the enemy—the terrorist. Are we not perpetuating the act of terrorism by reminding ourselves of terror? Rather, those who stood up against the horrific acts of terrorism, those who were out front should be what comes to mind, and who should be honored. How we served should define our generation, not who or what we fought against.

We as a nation should focus on this—and never forget that the Frontline Generation had the audacity to serve.

As I glanced in the rearview mirror and saw the innocent face of my son peacefully sleeping in the back seat, I knew that one day he would ask me about my time in the military and *the* global war on terror. With that revelation, a tinge of unmistakable duty overwhelmed me. I knew that calling all too well. At this point, my book was well on its way, but I was simply going to print it off on my home printer and hand it to my son one day.[8]

Seeing that road sign pushed me over. The time off I was taking to be with my son was about something more than I ever could have comprehended. I knew I should start now, to not wait for my son's questions; I should become an active participant in defining the narrative of my generation of service members. I wanted to choose what my generation would be called and how we would be remembered. After all, I had the frontline perspective—I am the 1 percent.

Veterans and others I witnessed firsthand from my Frontline Generation are unequivocally resilient people who sought purpose and took action. We are not perfect, but by and large the quality of the person was perfectly molded by our passion to serve. Like you, we've asked ourselves at one point (if not several) in our lives *who* did we want to be, *how* could we make a difference, how would our lives *count*? Although we surely answered those questions differently, service was, and is, the common denominator. My generation's legacy is rooted in our actions to volunteer and be exposed to the forefront of action, time and time again. And just like the Greatest Generation deserved and earned that title, my generation of service members equally deserves and earned ours—the Frontline Generation.

Because there were no real front lines. The people I served beside became them.

I decided at that moment my son should not be the only beneficiary of my distinct perspective as a post 9/11 veteran. Exactly because I am now a mother, I have a strong sense, an obligation, to share. Which, by the way, are the same lessons and qualities I would share if I had a daughter. With that, I have learned my time in the military not only shaped the person I am today, but also my hope for who my son will become. May these stories inform and inspire, as they illustrate how service is a force that gives us meaning. It can unite us, and can make us leaders.

INTRODUCTION

★ ★ ★

Fist Full of Glitter

On a cold morning in December of 2009, I met up with two of my sergeants from one of my thirteen teams at a main gate along the perimeter of Bagram Airfield, Afghanistan. My soldiers and I were filling a few empty seats on what was considered a routine patrol by an agriculture development team. The convoy and the mission had us stopping in Mahmud-i-Raqi, the village that is the crossroads to Main Supply Route (MSR) Nevada and MSR Vermont.

My joining the convoy on that morning served two purposes. One, I could observe my soldiers on a mission in which they were collecting information from everything on the local geography to people, in order to help solve the puzzle of *priority intelligence requirements*. Second, it would also give me a chance to do a route reconnaissance, since that was the same road I would take in a few days with a different intelligence team of mine scheduled to convoy to a French operations base in Kapisa Province.

On that particular day, the routes were considered a medium threat level, with some activity of small-arms fire but not really a threat for improvised explosive devices, known as IEDs, or roadside bombs. Nonetheless, a few additional MRAPs [mine-resistant ambush protected vehicles] were lined up at the front of the convoy, and their equipment and the unit patches on their uniforms immediately identified them as EOD—Explosives

Ordinance Disposal. Bomb detectors. Apparently, a local national had called in throughout the night, warning US forces an IED might be emplaced in a culvert along the route. Now, these types of tips are not uncommon, and not always accurate—yet all of them are taken seriously. The individual had even provided an approximate grid coordinate.

With more than fifty pounds of additional weight from my body armor, extra ammunition, and two locked and loaded weapons (an M9 Beretta and M4 rifle), I climbed into the second MRAP with Sergeant Jesse Miller, claiming the two empty seats in the back. I had known this blond, blue-eyed Texan for a few years, ever since he reported to my company fresh out of basic training. I had shaken his parents' hands a few months earlier at our farewell ceremony back home and told them I would take care of their son.

That responsibility felt heavier than it had ever been, since a few weeks earlier, on a similar brisk, early morning, we had paid our last respects to a fallen comrade at an unforgettable ramp ceremony—one who had lost his life when his MRAP drove over an IED. Jesse had helped carry the flag-draped coffin.

These were all things you try to not think about before a mission, and our mission was still a go. Jesse looked over at me and smiled as we left the relative safety of the base. I wondered if perhaps my impeccably bright soldier was more comfortable going "outside the wire" because he spoke Pashto. Being fluent in the native language would be pretty damn helpful right now, I thought. I stayed focused by listening to the occasional squawk or static from our headsets, as the truck commander provided constant updates on our progress.

It feels like forever when you're driving to a destination marked with an IED.

As our convoy neared the site, the lead truck in front of us came to an abrupt security halt, and over the radios I heard, "Oh shit, I think we passed the grid. The location is actually about a hundred meters behind us. All trucks, check if you have a culvert by you and do not stop near one."

Jesse and I looked out the bulletproof glass window in the back door of our MRAP, and lo and behold, a few feet behind our truck was a culvert . . .

THE NEED TO SHARE

I am a female veteran, one who served as a commander on the front lines. I have experienced the overpowering revelation that we truly do have *only* one life to live. During numerous, salient moments from ten years of post 9/11 service, I asked myself who I wanted to be, how I would help, and how my life would count. Extraordinary and unexpected answers were unearthed. Those answers were from my own story, and, more importantly, shown how *my* story was set against a backdrop of a groundbreaking generation of service members who faced challenges head on, charted new paths, and transformed military norms. The time that now separates my time in uniform has helped me more fully appreciate this unique background—and all that I learned from my Frontline Generation, lessons I need to share about life, leadership, and service.

I should also note that I feel compelled to write this because of how I have been wired. I am a product of the paradigm shift the intelligence community underwent after 9/11. I started my career with a generation of intelligence professionals who had the attitude that information is not something that should be held hostage on a need-to-know basis. Instead, I learned to look at information from the starting point of whether it would help or benefit a person (mission) if I *did* share.[9] Thus, there is something new to be said—and yet, sometimes all too familiar—about my generation's character, our sacrifice, and service.

Staying true to my professional ethos as a former military intelligence officer, I need to share what my remarkable generation and I did—how we served on the front lines.[10]

LEAVE A TRAIL

Could anyone have imagined 9/11 before it happened? I couldn't. Further, I certainly would never have believed that after 9/11 some in my generation would spend over a decade fighting a global war on terrorism in Afghanistan, Iraq, and elsewhere. Asymmetric warfare was the nature of this conflict, even before terrorists hijacked civilian planes on September 11, 2001, to the counterinsurgency operations that ensued on the streets of Baghdad and Kabul.[11] Therefore, unlike previous wars in which the front line was clearly defined, *anyone* who served in my generation could be exposed to the forefront of combat action.

And we were—starting with those in the military and extending to journalists, government officials, nongovernment workers, and contractors alike. Nevertheless, it was not what one did or where one served, whether convoying through Eastern Afghanistan or operating from a forward operations base (FOB). What made these people part of my Frontline Generation in this environment is *how* they served. They stepped up to volunteer in the first place and they helped post 9/11, knowing they would all, undeniably, be out front and in harm's way. That act of service took character— and it was meaningful in ways one could never dream.

My Frontline Generation included women too. Like you, I never could have anticipated what history *will* definitively pronounce as what was *noticeably different* in these wars—that such a large number of females were among the ranks of those serving out front. Up until my generation it was a *known unknown,* as I would describe it in tribute to Secretary of Defense Donald Rumsfeld's infamous quote.[12] The US military did not really know how women would fare as leaders on the front lines, in combat—it had never been observed to the extent it would be after 9/11. That unknown was eradicated almost instantly when the front lines blurred . . . dissolved. Retired General Peter Chiarelli, who served as the 32nd Vice Chief of Staff of the United States Army from 2008 to 2012 said it concisely, "Women have participated in conflict for hundreds of years . . . but these wars are different. From the time you entered in the countries of Iraq or Afghanistan, you were in harm's way, whether you were male or female."[13]

Circumstances thus advanced a woman's right to equal opportunity—equal exposure to combat.

Consequently, there are now thousands of women who have set the bar. And I was one of those women. Therefore, this book is rooted in the perspective of being out front as a member of the military—even as a woman—and it shares the story of those in my generation who were alongside me, those who left an indelible mark on not only my heart, but also on history. We served all *together* in this new territory, with no clear preexisting path. And we left a trail.

TAKING ON LIFE

Thus the best way I can help define my Frontline Generation is by walking you through the history I lived. You will learn that what initially drove me to step into this male-dominated world after 9/11 was my sincere desire to serve in uniform, plain and sim-ple. My plan of action to becoming successful in this endeavor is outlined, in addition to sharing the hurdles and collisions with many antagonists along the way—from men, women, the hier-archical military system, all the way to the elements of being in combat. Along the way, several confrontations led me to the self-revelation that what I wanted was not what I needed. I *wanted* to serve but *needed* to grow, as a person and as a leader.

What further differentiates this book is that several of the lessons are in their original form—because most were captured through a heartfelt daily journal I kept while deployed to Afghanistan.[14] Although the journal started out as a way for me to write letters to my husband when the Internet and phones were down, it evolved as a means to shelve my hopes and fears as a commander, to sort out the range of emotions I felt while deployed to combat, and, most importantly, to collect the stories of my remarkable soldiers so that I would never forget them.[15] Because those stories are lessons that gave me hope and empowered me.

Fundamentally, they taught me how to live. How to *really* live.

Thus you will learn the personalities of those I served with, the challenges we faced, and inspirations that helped us make it through the day.[16] The journal entries provide real-time reaction. They are peppered with the realities of a combat deployment and what only struggle can so abruptly reveal. Some days cover the raw details of being in Afghanistan, others offer extracts of missions, frustrations with those around me, and prayers I said to God that night.[17] What every journal entry has in common is an honest depiction of my Frontline Generation, offered through the lens of this individual—a female leader and a combat veteran.

Finally, by reading about the range of people who served, you may be encouraged that you, too, are capable of serving with honor, of leading with distinction, in whatever capacity you so choose. You, too, can take on life. My story occurred while I was in the army, but the lessons can be applied to any position in society or the workforce. That is because so many of the issues I dealt with as a leader in the army are real everywhere. I am not shy about addressing the more difficult topics either, such as post-traumatic stress, suicide, sexual assault, female integration, "don't ask, don't tell," stop-loss, loss of life, and more.

By the end of this book, you will have experienced the ability to withstand hardship, how the ordinary turned into extraordinary, how unprecedented challenges were surmounted, and how navigating the unexpected became the expected. And, that *close calls* don't discriminate when you drive over IEDs on cold December mornings.

After each chapter, a short note will be inserted (in italics, like this). This is the fist full of glitter. These lessons are the strong, bright, and shimmering light that I want to give back. They reflect my sincere hopes for the next generation (my son), and they are what distinguish my Frontline Generation.

PART 1: THE ROAD TO COMMAND

★ ★ ★

You Have a Choice

In the army, soldiers know that all the really good stories start with, "No shit, there I was . . ." It didn't take me long to realize the "no shit" caveat was to emphasize that this would be a ridiculously wild story. Just the same, I had a calm and steady staff sergeant, Brad Schmidt (Schmitty), who would come into my office while we were deployed, shaking his head, and would begin nearly every conversation with, "Ma'am, I can't make this shit up."

Looking back on my ten years of service in the army, which includes two combat deployments, I, too, shake my head and think, *So there I was* . . . My inconceivable journey, which culminated in a company command in Afghanistan, began as soon as I started basic training in the early spring of 2002.

I can still hear his bark, riddled with a southern drawl, and can see the spray of spit that escaped his mouth when he ordered us to stand at attention. He was tall, dark, and quite a bit scary. He was one of my drill sergeants. And I crossed his path on day one. It had been a long day of in-processing and trying to remember all the new rules, from how to stand and salute, to always having another soldier of the same gender with you wherever you went (the vaunted battle-buddy system). I had to go to the bathroom and thought I could quickly sneak away from the group, which was waiting outside the chow hall for dinner. Needless to say, that didn't work out so well.

"Soldier, where the hell are you going and where the hell is your battle buddy?"

I stopped abruptly and turned to see this beast of a man heading right at me, center mass. I stood at attention, addressed him accordingly, and thought, *No problem, I'll calmly explain to him I have to use the restroom and I forgot to bring a battle buddy.*

No. First, I was corrected on my word choice, because restrooms are called latrines. As it happened, it was one of those moments when you feel like you are outside your body watching your life happen to you: I *smiled* at him when he corrected my word choice. Bad, bad idea. Then it began.

"Oh, you want to smile at me. You are going to be one of those types of females."

I snapped, "What do mean one of *those* types of females? I was just thinking how funny this situation is. I simply used the wrong word."

"Oh, funny, huh?" He laid into me with a diatribe I will never forget.

"Nothing is funny about this situation. I need to reeducate your civilian mind to think like a soldier and know that you do not forget. You do not forget your battle buddy. If you are not disciplined in small things, you will not be disciplined in big things, like not forgetting your rifle somewhere later on. Oh, and, what I meant by one of *those* types of females is that you have a decision to make right now. There are three types of females in the army. Your smiling at me only makes me think you are hitting on me, so I know what option you chose."

At this point, he saw my jaw drop open in shock and my face turn red with anger. He kept going.

"Now you're getting mad. That's good, unless you turn butch on me and make every thing about proving yourself. My *job* is to make you a *bitch*. Do you understand me? Now get back in the chow hall line with your platoon."

I can count the number of times in my life that I've been speechless, and the number of times in my life I simply wanted to punch someone in the face. This moment was both. Thank God the shock of that confrontation froze my gut reaction. I returned to the chow hall a different person.

I was twenty-two years old at the time, college educated, and a proud owner of a passport with a few stamps in it. Hard-working, blue-collar parents raised me, and I worked several jobs myself to pay my way through school. Even then I was focused and goal-oriented, I did not live my life to prove anything.[18] I had a job back home in beautiful Southern California, and did not have to be there. That drill sergeant did not know me. My friends and family would describe me as highly disciplined, naturally happy, with a warm and ready smile. Evidently, I was not ready for the army.

Contemplating his words while lying in my bunk that night, I resolved the battle with him would be semantics. His job was to make me a soldier and that is all I would allow him to do. Besides, this was now my army too. I wanted to serve in uniform, and no one would intimidate me with sexist or undeserved stereotypes, which are all around us. The only way to debunk them is to live your life in contrast to them. As time would unveil, several exchanges in my future would test my resolve and grace, and those would not only be as a soldier and leader in combat, but here at home, in boardrooms and at universities.

Every person will face hurdles; we must all overcome something. This is life. For me, at that moment, I could prevail if I stayed in the army, exactly where I wanted to be, and become a soldier. I would turn this table—and sit at the table; the army would not be ready for me.

I decided that night I had more than three choices on what type of female I would be in the army. In fact, I knew this man was not aware that he, as a man, does not have the right to tell me, as a woman, what kind of woman I will be—drill sergeant or not. He had a lot to learn about women—especially this one. Giving him the benefit of the doubt, I translated his message to mean this: I sensed he was trying to articulate that he wanted me to be tough, and to be there for the right reasons, which was not to find a husband, or wife, or to prove myself. He wanted me to be committed to the soldier next to me. He wanted me to have army values, to be my best, because someone else now counted on me. His or her life would depend on me. The stakes are at their highest in uniform.

I would come to understand that all too well during my ten years in uniform. That drill sergeant never knew that I would go on to serve two combat tours, one in support of Operation Iraqi Freedom, the other in support of Operation Enduring Freedom in Afghanistan. I would start out enlisted, receive the rare honor of being awarded a direct commission, climb the ranks as an officer, and ultimately become a company commander. My final duty was to lead over one hundred soldiers in Afghanistan to successfully fulfill their mission and safely return home. Those stakes were, indeed, the highest.

I did not begrudge (or excuse) him for his rude, politically incorrect, ill-informed, expletive-laced tirades. The truth is I would still want to smile and laugh today if he corrected my word choice. For me, smiling easily was (is) a habit hard to break. My mom taught me when I was a little girl to even smile during difficult times, to include when I was mad at someone, because, as she claimed, it would drive the other person nuts wondering why I was still smiling. My mom's advice was not particularly helpful with drill sergeants, but a token of power I keep today.

In fact, over the remaining twelve weeks of basic training, that drill sergeant would stop me regularly and tell me to drop and do ten push-ups because I looked like I wanted to smile. Sure enough, I would look at the ground, and smile to my heart's content as I did those push-ups. He would give me the tools to be a soldier; I would make the conscious decision to be a good soldier, which would help set the foundation for me to become a great commander.[19] That drill sergeant was doing the best he knew how to harden us and turn us into soldiers. And we were soldiers who would most likely serve in combat. Our nation was at war.

Do not let anyone else define you.

Remember that you decide what kind of person you will be. Review the available options, and if you don't like those that are given—be bold and create your own.

If you want to join the military, that will be your choice too. Yet my hope (and prayer) is you will never have to serve in a time of war.

Passion Chase

I was there for the right reasons—I cared. That gruff drill sergeant that I had in basic training did not know that I joined the military after 9/11, because of 9/11. I was starting from a place of purpose, cause, and belief. Our nation had just experienced the worst terrorist attack in its history, and I was well aware from my newly minted bachelor's degree in political science that we had just spent the previous decade reducing the size of the force. I understood that our future as a nation would change, from foreign to domestic policy, and I wanted to be an active participant in my generation's story. Joining the military was the right way for me to serve at that moment in time.

Service can be compared to that road that you find in every town—the one that changes names as you drive along it. You know, it will start out as Main Street, and then turns into Highway 49, and before you know it you see signs that you are driving on Hillsboro Road. All one and the same are the words *service, passion, cause, belief, conviction,* and *love*. There are many others words that can be supplemented to fit on this same road but these are the more common words you will read in my journal entries and stories, and it is important for you to know up front that they can be interchangeable in how I use them.

Most importantly is my belief that service is a road we must all find in our lives. When I found my road named "Army," it changed my life for the good. Furthermore, serving helped me become the leader I never imagined I could be.

Examine your heart and start with what matters to you. (Anyone can do this.) That is how I know that my motives are grounded in service. In the spring of 2001, I had an American flag pinned to the top of my black mortarboard when I graduated from college. I put it there to symbolize the American Dream, since I was one of the first in my family to attend a four-year university and only the second to earn a college degree.[20] The flag was also there to symbolize my major, political science, which was an area of study that had intrigued me from my earliest childhood memories. If I close my eyes, I can look back and see myself as a little girl sitting cross-legged on the carpet in front of my parents' box-style television, watching the fall of the Berlin Wall on NBC. By the fall of 2001, it was no surprise that I needed to wear another American flag, this time on camouflage.[21]

It probably wasn't a surprise to my parents, either. They were proud, but decidedly unhappy about my decision to join the military. I am from a large family and rarely have one-on-one time with them; they knew something was up when I asked them to meet me for breakfast at Denny's so we could talk.[22] I remember my mom saying, "But you have a degree, you shouldn't have to go."

My mother was coming from a different generation's point of view—the Vietnam Generation.[23] Her brothers were drafted, and at one time, four of them were serving combat tours in Vietnam. Going into the military is what poor families would do, from her experience.[24] She was from a large Midwestern family that worked on farms to earn a living; she knew all too well how hard life could be. Her siblings used the military as a way to get out and on their own, since there was hardly enough money to put food on the table, let alone for a higher education. She was immensely proud of my recent graduation from college, and I tried to reassure her that my college education was exactly why I should serve in the military, and that I was not stepping backwards.[25]

Additionally, I told her that I wanted to do this, that I was joining an all-volunteer force. She was quiet for a while, staring into her cup of coffee, but finally looked up at me with her gentle eyes and said, "Well, at least you will go in as an officer with your college degree." That's when I had to break the news to her that I was signing a service obligation to be an enlisted soldier. Needless to say, any ground that I had made with her was lost, and she was totally upset and opposed to my decision all over again. I assured her that I had plenty of time to become an officer, but that I wanted to start my service in uniform as an enlisted soldier. She argued with me vigorously: "You are setting yourself up for failure—you have always been a leader, from senior class president to captain of the volleyball team. Plus, you have your father's mouth on you—you'll speak up and get in trouble."

This is when my dad, who had been unusually quiet during this entire conversation, interjected. "Marlene, you do not have to have a title to be a leader. She will be a leader as an enlisted soldier, and this will be good for her in that sense because it will teach her to keep her mouth shut. She will be a better leader because she will know how to follow."[26] My father does not mince his words, or filter much thought either. He is a cowboy, a union man, who has always had a flagpole in his yard and keeps his draft card in his bedside stand to this day. He would have loved to serve in uniform, and was officially on the books for a couple of days until he was disqualified for medical reasons. He would have been a terrific soldier, sailor, airman, or marine. He is no less a patriot, and loves his country.

He looked at me and said, "Okay. If that is your decision, okay. Just keep your head down because you're awfully tall to be out front. Now, are you getting pancakes or biscuits?"

Make a decision and don't look back.
Do not be afraid to live.

The chase is not a race. It's a road
with many names. Take it.

May your passion be being a part of the solution.

The dreams and desires in your heart are
there for a reason. Believe in them. Besides,
God would not have put them there without
giving you the talents to achieve them.

Service can be the biggest springboard
to unearthing one's interest.

★ ★ ★

Patriotic Guilt

In 2005, the *Los Angeles Times* ran an editorial called "Patriotic Guilt"[27] and I have never been so put off by such an arrogant musing and nonchalant judgment of those who served in my post 9/11 generation.

"What if," the author muses, "my parents hadn't gone into debt to provide me with a private school education and the benefits it affords? What if, instead, I had taken the path followed by many in my hometown and pursued my American dream through the military?"

The more I read, the angrier I got, as the writer blithely dismissed, in general, the motives and intentions of 1.5 millions US soldiers serving at that time and, specifically, one from his own hometown.

> *Now, I'm sure a fair number of those in the military enlisted out of a lack of other options. I know full well that relatively few in my generation buy into the "for flag and country" bit, and that my sense of patriotic guilt would probably make for a good joke or two in the service. And the honest truth is that nothing less than a full-fledged draft could get me to say goodbye to my wife's puppy-dog brown eyes and put on a uniform.*

Maybe I just lack the conviction of the soldiers deployed in Iraq. Or maybe they've just lacked my good fortune.

You can find the entire op/ed online.

I sent a response to the paper, but it was never printed. Nevertheless, it will forever capture my conviction on service, which is the undercurrent to the character of my Frontline Generation. If I could speak directly to the writer, this is what I'd say:

Mr. Rawls, you began your editorial on "Patriotic Guilt" by exploiting a sad truth of war—post-traumatic stress (PTS). Everybody is affected in some way when deployed to combat; yet not everyone suffers from PTS or to the extent in which you described. A more fitting introduction to your piece would have been you drinking yourself silly and screaming you were going to kill yourself because the regret you'll feel one day for not fighting when you were able, for not fighting before we were attacked again.

The resounding query you pose is whether you lack the conviction of soldiers in Iraq or if they lack your good fortune. Although all I know of you is from what you described in your editorial, I believe I have your answer.

The soldiers in Iraq or in uniform do not lack your good fortune. You lack ours.

I have been blessed with an incredible education. From the UC system to studies abroad in London (mind you that somewhere in between I was also selected as a White House intern), I clearly did not "lack other options" in the fall of 2001. I set my graduate school applications aside to serve my country in its time of need. You may tag me as one of the relatively few in our generation who buys into "for flag and country," yet I'll have you know I've bought nothing. I believe in serving. And I challenge you and the rest of our "generation" to heed the call to service made by a particular favorite role model of mine, who once said, "Ask not what your country can do for you, ask what you can do for your country." Oren, our country needs us—all of us—more than ever.

Perhaps your reason enough in not serving is your contention with the current government. Mr. Rawls, I was not interning when "W" was in the Oval Office, so you do the political math. You do not have to subscribe to a political side in choosing to wear the uniform. Engineers, journalists, nurses, and civil affairs servants of all sorts are nation building right now—not Republicans, Democrats, or Independents. Just Americans! Furthermore, a tremendous amount of these patriots have a civilian career and give when called; the reserves may be the best option for you.

Why do you think you have "not had to" strap on boots? The honorable service from three generations of your family ensured your freedoms, even the one that allows you not to serve or even burn the flag.

But everything is different now; we were attacked. Have you asked yourself what will happen if you do not put those boots on this generation? Will it be worse for the next—your children? You have clearly taken the opportunities this wonderful land provides you, but what have you given? Now, service is not only warranted when in uniform, so have you been a teacher or a member of the Peace Corp yet? What are you giving back to this country? Just in case you missed it, right now our country especially needs the service of soldiers, sailors, airmen, and marines.

When you state that you "look the part," I would like to redirect your notion of what "the part" looks like. A soldier looks like a man or woman who emits personal courage, selflessness, one with a sense of duty and loyalty. These are the traits that I see in my husband, an army helicopter pilot, and those that he says he admires in me. When we have been separated by combat deployments, although nothing makes it easy to say good-bye to his true blue eyes, I cherish our good fortune as soldiers—believing and serving in something bigger than oneself. Find your conviction, Mr. Rawls.

—M. K. Eastman, veteran

*Anyone and everyone can serve in some way.
It is a hands-on, immediate, selfless act that can be
fulfilled individually or collectively.*

*By the way, there is no gender, age, height, or (fill in
the blank) requirement when it comes to service.*

Find your conviction.

★ ★ ★

Sometimes All You Should Do Is Smile

Have you ever been in a small group, and the person in charge asks to go around the room and have people introduce themselves? Most of us have, right? Well, this is how almost every graduate school class began at the Josef Korbel School of International Studies when I attended from the fall of 2006 until my graduation in the summer of 2008. It was about midway through my program of study, while introducing myself in one of these circles, when I had another one of those unforgettable exchanges that involved a smile.

I knew the drill—state your name, major, and something interesting about yourself. They were small classes, approximately two dozen students, and most of us had already met and knew of each other. So generally we kept to the script, and this process moved along fairly quickly, without interruption. After all, this ring-around-the-rosy was really for the professor.

Heads around the room are following the person speaking. Next, next, next . . . Let's keep this moving. My turn. Ready, go.

"I am Marjorie Eastman, my major is International Security, and I am a veteran."

My friend Jessica, who was sitting next to me, started in with her introduction, but was stopped.

"Wait." The professor held up his hand. He was still looking at me.

Up to this point, he hadn't said anything to anyone. He had only given us guidance to go around the room with the introductions, and had been nodding along.

"You are a veteran? What branch of service and what war?"

Now, I had read his biography before class and knew he had been drafted during Vietnam and served in the air force. I didn't expect he'd want to be chatty, or confrontational, about my mention of being a veteran. I wasn't sure what to expect now, since the tone of his questions were piercing.

"I am still in the US Army Reserve and I was deployed in 2003 in support of Operation Iraqi Freedom."

He was sitting, rather leaning halfway on a desk, front and center of the classroom. He maintained eye contact, and I watched him slowly digest my response. After a momentary pause, he asked another question, which I can only describe as either awkwardly erudite or snide.

"Iraq. Well, yes, then, do tell us, how did you enjoy your travels over there?"

Travels? What was he talking about? I didn't go on some all-inclusive paid vacation or sightseeing expedition. I knew he understood I was on a deployment because he asked me what war. I was cautious with his leading question. Veterans are those who serve in uniform, not just those who have served in war. I was not going to play this game of trying to guess what he meant, so I quickly decided to ask a clarifying question.

I said, "Travels?"

"Yes, your travels, your trip. Did you enjoy your time in Meso-potamia?"

Okay. By this point, I was convinced he was being both awkwardly erudite and snide.

I replied with my best attempt to diffuse his interest. "I would have preferred to be there under different conditions."

He smirked and with a broadening grin (as if to laugh before telling his own joke), he said, "Why yes, that's because it is Mess-opotamia. And, we made it a bigger *mess*."

We? We made it a bigger mess? There is nothing that my direct, German Shepherd side hates more than when a loose pronoun with no ownership is thrown like a bone. I wanted to pounce on him with my own list of questions: Do you mean *we*, as in the majority of Congress who voted to send troops over there, or *we*, as in the intelligence community who put too much weight on a sole source, or we, as in the *Coalition of the Willing* who found the premise for war just, or *we*, as in me, the soldier who was sent over there? Which we do you mean? And, how about the we who objected to the war, who did not find a way to change the course of history?

The world is all about we, isn't it?

Did he anticipate my response to be riddled with theory on mankind's human nature, or for me to acknowledge the seminal shift in national security policy post 9/11 and the vir-tues and consequences of preemptive versus preventive? Should I have offered my insight as a trained intelligence officer, or pro-vide a first-account experience of the dirt on my boots? Perhaps he wanted to get into the hot topic of the day, the surge of troops in Iraq, and share with the class the personal toll of that decision, since I am a spouse of a surge soldier who was on an extended fifteen-month combat tour flying close air support Apache

Longbow helicopters—every day—over a very kinetic (would he say *messy*?) Sadr City.

I resisted the urge to turn it around, and I did not stick a finger in his chest or preach about the "mess" his generation made. No. I don't know what he went through, just as he didn't know what I had been through—or what was still on my shoulders.

Besides, soldiers do not choose the wars they fight—policymakers do. *We* all need to remember that.

What did I do? I looked right back into his eyes and gave him a warm smile. And, just as my mom had said, I had the power. He probably thought I enjoyed his clever play on words. He smiled back, turned to the next person and nodded. The procession of introductions continued. I stopped listening and internalized what had just happened. Mesopotamia, huh? He had no idea.

People make assumptions all the time. Be careful not to do this. Further, be patient and display grace with those that do.

One of my soldiers told me once, "Ma'am, I know why you are always smiling. People are no different from most every other mammal that shows its teeth before it bites."

Never be deceived that smiling is a weakness (especially if you are a woman). When done effectively, it is quite the contrary.

★ ★ ★

Chart Your Own Path

I enlisted in the United States Army Reserve in February of 2002. By September of that same year, I had completed basic training and my advanced initial training for my occupational specialty. I eagerly reported for my first drill weekend with my new reserve unit in October of 2002, and it was the next month, in November, that my unit would be activated. Almost exactly a year to the day that I raised my right hand and took an oath to serve my country, my country called upon me to serve in combat.

My activation orders started out with some vague but key term that I was being ordered to active duty and mobilized to support the Global War on Terror (GWOT). It wasn't until I had already seen the sunset over the Arabian Desert that my mission became known as Operation Iraqi Freedom (OIF). I was with the first wave of soldiers, or OIF I.[28] This would be the first of my two combat deployments, and although both Iraq and Afghanistan fall under the overarching GWOT term, OIF was arguably the first of two very different wars in which I would serve.

I was the only female activated from my reserve company, and that was clearly not the preference of the man in charge. I was supposed to *only* be a token female who would remain on the alternate list, because the old man did not want problems, I'd heard. I was already enough of a hassle because even as an alternate they had to find female accommodations or openly discuss if my female medical exams were taken care of. As another seasoned soldier explained it to me, it was probably worse than being a "dirty leg" (which is when you are not airborne qualified) since my very presence required them to say words like *annual pap smear*. Thus, once my status changed on the battle roster list to being a soldier who would deploy, I knew I was being pulled along not because I was considered an asset—a soldier—it was because others had fallen off the battle roster for injuries, medical issues, or not passing physical fitness standards. It was a demeaning, inferior place to start when being sent to war. I felt all alone.

All I knew of the people in my unit was what you can learn in the brutal weeks of a mobilization period—which can be best described as "hurry up and wait." You are shuffled through multiple buildings and training sites during this soldier readiness process (SRP) on a large army installation. In 2003, my reserve company was sent to process through Ft. Bragg, North Carolina. From qualifying on your weapon to filling out paperwork for a will, life insurance, and power of attorney, it seems like an endless checklist of requirements must be completed before you are sent overseas. "Good enough," often prevailed, as I learned the day that I was issued desert boots—a size too large for my feet. Over the next several months (in the hot desert), I would wear two, sometimes three pairs of thick socks in order to keep my feet from sliding in my boots and causing blisters.[29]

Yes, to be sent to Mesopotamia under different conditions—with boots that fit—would have been my preference.

Just days before movement, I was attached to support a Special Operations Task Force with a handful of other soldiers from my reserve unit. It was all the same to me—I did not know any of them and we were all heading to the same place, via different bases.

At least the unit I would now support had a few other females. The overwhelming feeling of loneliness was ever present, though.

I was enlisted, young, and had only been in the Army for about a year when I walked onto the ramp of an enormous C5 aircraft heading to the Middle East. And I had never felt so uncertain about my life as I did in that moment. It must have been written all over my face, because the senior noncommissioned officer in charge of my team approached me.

"How are you holding up?" asked Sergeant First Class Jack Hughes.

I clenched my teeth and blinked rapidly, trying to fight back tears and muster a steady voice to speak the lie, "Good, sergeant."

Sergeant Hughes was an overly serious-looking man (think George Clooney), an impression one would naturally derive from his full head of gray hair and inquisitive brow that was stuck in place probably from giving one too many depositions. He was a lawyer from Orange County, one who loved being a soldier on the weekends because he "got to jump out of airplanes and sleep in tents." The more I came to know him throughout our activation, his easygoing and relaxed California demeanor would sneak out. Yet I was intimidated (which doesn't happen often), because of this new thing the army had pounded into my head—rank.

He read me like the shifting, squirmy juror that I was, and said, "Hey, I want you to know that you're going to do fine over there. I wouldn't have asked the commander to put you on my team otherwise."

He stood up for me? He wanted me on his team? I was stunned—but more importantly, uplifted—by his genuine admission. He must have read that on my face too.

"Just let me know if you need something. I know you've got a big brain in that Kevlar. What you don't know, you'll figure out." And with that, he walked away.

I'll figure it out. Those words rang in my ears.

In order to figure it out, I began writing in a small notebook, on that gray whale of a C5, the night we departed Ft. Bragg. The notebook quickly became a journal, my refuge and secret garden of hopes, fears, and dreams. The notes I kept during OIF started out as a way for me to process all the emotions, so many of them new, that I was experiencing while being deployed. As weeks turned into months, my small notebook turned into something else—something more.

My OIF journal became a "smart book," a list of lessons on how I wanted to be as a soldier, as a leader, and the change I wished to see in the world (and army). From things that I saw done right, to those that were done terribly wrong, from leadership examples, operation successes, to life lessons that would all contribute to my becoming the best soldier that I could be. I wrote about all of them in that notebook.

The idea of a smart book originated for me in basic training. Remember that gruff drill sergeant? He also ordered the soldiers in my platoon to always keep a small notebook and pen in one of our uniform pockets so that we could write down useful "army things," like the maximum range of our rifle and how to find coordinates on a map. During those hurry-up-and-wait moments in basic training, he would bark at us to pull out our smart books and get smart (study). These notebooks were also required to have the Soldier's Creed and Army Values in them. So there I was, just a little over a year from basic training, sitting in the Middle East, writing in my smart book every day. Getting smart. By the time I returned home from my OIF deployment, I had an outline of a plan on how to move forward in my army career.

This was the first step I took, and it helped me "arrive before I arrived" in Afghanistan years later as a commander. And from that point on, I kept an eye out for solid examples (often of noncommissioned officers like Hughes) to guide me. And, in essence, allow them to do so, and to look out for me. With all that said, I began the thoughtful preparation—and overpreparation—to becoming the leader that I wanted to follow.

Trailblazers make sense of the unknown in life by charting their own paths. Do not wait for someone to give you a map.

Further, expect that nearly every path in life will have to be traveled with sand in your boots, which probably will not fit you, either.

Taking off tends to require going against the wind.[30]

★ ★ ★

Collect and Wear Pearls of Wisdom

"There is sand everywhere!" I said out loud. Needlessly.

Mary just smiled, nodded her head in agreement, and kept cleaning.

We were shaking and wiping off everything, then sweeping up piles of sand. It looked like someone had walked through our tent with several bags of sand and dumped them out. Our cots, our sleeping bags, our tough boxes, and even our towels that had been hanging from posts that framed the inside of our tent—everything was covered in sand. Yet no one had maliciously played such a horrible prank. Thankfully those sandbags that were stacked around the outside of our tent had held it down the night before when a horrendous sandstorm called a *shamal* reeked havoc on our small, remote base.

Mary slept on the cot across from mine, in that drab brown tent that we shared with a handful of additional lower-ranked enlisted females who were also on my forward operations base near Iraq. And we all took turns cleaning, since our shifts varied, and absolutely appreciated the fact that the tent indeed was fortified enough at the base with sandbags to help, at best, secure it from flying away during one of the many sandstorms we endured while deployed. The journal entry I have of Mary and I cleaning together on that particular day was a reminder that she was a reoccurring name in my OIF journal. That was because she was an awesome example of one of the types of women I aspired to be like while wearing a uniform.

The funny aspect of this is, she was not in the military—she was a defense contractor. As a *female* contractor, which was why she was in the "enlisted female" tent with me and a handful of others. She who had no rank was bunking with us who had little rank. Nevertheless, Mary made a remarkable impact on us, day after day. She could have been Mother Mary in disguise, for all I know. She truly was a saint to me.

It was her kindness in the midst of all the chaos that initially resonated with me; she would ask if I had eaten for the day, check on me to see if I needed extra batteries for my headlamp, and listen to me lament about some of the individuals I worked with or how much I missed my family and friends back home. Her calm comments were like pearls of wisdom I began to collect. Her kindness, interestingly, did not insinuate she was weak, either. She was composed, steady, no fuss, and level-headed. What made her especially fun to watch is that she was nonchalant about all the rigidity that surrounded us.

Further, I guarantee no one could ever have guessed what her occupation was, as she was five foot nothing, older, probably had not run a mile in years, and for the most part, would be tagged as a kindergarten teacher. Yet she was performing a vital role providing intelligence support to a Special Operations Task Force and serving in the Middle East. Her reputation preceded her as one of the best analysts in her field. Moreover, she also made it her job to help others, especially those who were perhaps facing the same challenges (I watched her "mother-hen" and look out for several of us female soldiers). I sense she took Madeleine Albright seriously when she said, "There is a special place in hell for women who do not help other women."

I would say this applies to people who just don't help others who share their same circumstances.

That was not Mary, though. She was kind and competent—and absolutely helped. I couldn't resist the desire to emulate her leadership style. And because I was a future intelligence professional, she subtly beat into my head the need to be ferociously objective and to look at everything from every perspective, realizing that most people fail miserably at both of those tasks. Especially in regular, day-to-day life. She taught all of this through *small talk*, nudging you to consider how others interpret the world around them from their perspective—and perception was reality, regardless if it was or not.

That nudge normally felt something like this:

"Mary, I'm going to take a break from cleaning and see if Chuck wants to go grab a schawarma for lunch. Do you want to join us, or can I bring something back for you?"

"That sounds good," Mary replied. "I've got to get back to the JOC [joint operations center], so don't worry about me. I'll grab something to eat on my way. *Are you going by yourself?*"

This is how she would nudge. Granted, it was the middle of the day, only going to the edge of the base with a trusted friend, yet Mary helped me see what a harmless twenty-minute trip to grab food (alone, with a male) might look like to others. It was this strange environment we were in that led to unnecessary mental meanderings like that. Devastating uncertainty in tough circumstances was pretty much our baseline—and a preponderance of inadequately apprising subordinates fed this monster. Uncertainty—in the Army and especially on a deployment—combined with boredom can lead a wild imagination to run amok and create what has been coined RUMINT (rumor intelligence). RUMINT was perpetuated despite how false the information truly was; if the gossip was about an individual, I learned it was typically started out of spite for that person.

By accident, both the positive examples and the adversity that I experienced during my OIF deployment did just that, and it all began to develop me as a soldier (and as a person). There were others who inspired me by their positive examples and influenced me to believe that I, too, could be a grain of sand that irritates the oyster to produce a pearl. I decided I would be kind, like Mary. I elected to not form an opinion from what things looked like. And I knew I needed to strive every day to grow and learn, to keep filling up that proverbial competency bucket.

I would also start employing the pearls of wisdom as soon as possible. There is a saying in the army that the "commander sets the tone." Although at that point I did not know that one day I would become a commander, I translated that idiom to mean that leaders set the tone, and every person regardless of rank or position could be a leader. I learned this because Mary was a leader. She set the tone, in her own sphere, which influenced others.

I concluded from my OIF experience that I would carry myself as a leader, as a commander, from that moment forward. Despite having no rank or position to support the mind-set, I would still behave in that manner and set the tone within my own sphere of influence. I started immediately implementing the behaviors and applying the lessons I was collecting on my string of pearls.

I began to look every person in the eye, give people the benefit of the doubt, and really pay attention (listen) to them. I'll never forget how sad one of the soldiers looked when he shared with me that no one in his chain of command remembered his birthday. He was on my team while we were deployed, and I understood how one can already feel so far away from normalcy that something which has meaning back home feels especially void when it is forgotten while deployed. This was the single reason why six years later I carried a list of all my soldiers' birthdays in my pocket when I was deployed as a commander, and I made a special effort to wish them well on their day.

The most significant lesson (pearl) I learned in the Middle East in 2003, for all those Groundhog days—where the same day repeats until the lesson is learned—is that first and foremost, a soldier would not respect a commander (or officer, or any other soldier for that matter) if his or her foundation was not built on competency. Like Mary's was. I wanted the first thing to be said about me to be, "She knows what she is doing . . . she knows what she is talking about." After that, let the adjectives pour in. And, as Mary taught me, we should strive for one of those adjectives to be *kind*.

Choose to become a pearl instead of remaining a grain of sand. You'll be much happier in life, even if it's the hard route.

Therefore, find an oyster to irritate; don't merely remain sand in someone's boot.

You do not have to have a title to be a leader. When you step up to serve, you are taking the first step to becoming a leader.

Yes Men and No Men

Taking advantage of all available training is generally a good tactic. Expect the unexpected in what you think you will need to be prepared for in life. After my OIF deployment, I returned to Ft. Bragg only to be told that I had to stay on active duty orders for the remainder of the year. During those several months, I signed up for every type of available training course on that installation. One course in particular that I knew would be important to attend was SERE (Survive, Escape, Resist, Evade), which is the Army's staple survival course that is typically filled with Special Forces soldiers (as it is a requirement for their baseline training). It had only been months since the Jessica Lynch story consumed the nightly news, and I was fully aware that women were just as vulnerable as men to be captured and taken as prisoners of war.

This course was always backlogged, with stringent requirements on who could fill the openings. At the time, I was fulfilling an occupational specialty (job position), which allowed me to at least be considered for it. Yet there was still that backlog. I learned from the active duty unit that I was attached to at Ft. Bragg that the way around that was to show up to the early morning role call on the first day of the course. If the class was not full due to unexpected drops from the roster, you could be accepted to attend the course.

The first morning I showed up, all of my gear meticulously pre-pared, taped, and in tow, I learned there were two openings. But there were three people hoping to "crash" the course. The noncommissioned officer in charge (NCOIC) came over to us and asked what our military occupational specialties were. All three of us had those second-tier job positions, which would help qualify our request to be admitted to the course, and I was higher-ranking than one of them, so I thought I had a chance. Without even looking at us, the sergeant barked the other two names—both males—as being added to the roster and then turned and walked away.

My first-line supervisor was with me that morning, and he went up to the NCOIC and asked why I wasn't selected, since rank was often a determining factor for those decisions. I was standing a couple of feet from both of them, and heard the NCOIC say (since these types of individuals do not tend to have indoor voices), "Females will not need this training as much as males because they are not on the front lines." My sergeant began to argue with him, telling him that my position would require me to be on pa-trols as a support element and that I was in a highly deployable position. The NCOIC cut him short, told him the decision was made, and walked away.

My sergeant was an optimist, though, and shared with me one of those classic Army sayings I had not yet heard: "There is a yes man and a no man, and you've just got to find the yes man." We planned to try the entire process all over again a couple of weeks later, in hopes that a different NCOIC would be making the call on who could be selected for the open slots. Again, early one morn-ing, I showed up for roll call. And who was standing out front with the check-in sheet—that same NCOIC. The circumstances were exactly the same, and again, he selected the other (male) soldiers. This time, my first-line supervisor was not with me, so I decided to confront the NCOIC and ask why I was not considered. He stared at me blankly as I made my case, then blurted out, "Sorry, toots, you are not getting into this course."

He was loud enough for all the other Special Forces soldiers around us to hear, and a low snicker rang in my ears. I was so humiliated! That moment taught me that although I could strive to attain the training, education, experience, and so on to become competent, there would be some people who would not see past my gender. Unfortunately, some of the gatekeepers were people like this. They were simply the no men who do not see past any number of things. Any rebuttal would have only made the situation worse with this man (even if it would temporarily make me feel better). Besides, who uses the term *toots*, anyway? I grabbed my rucksack and duffel, and I left. I would find another avenue of approach to acquire this training.

I remained passionate when the door closed on me. That included not letting that exchange temper my opinion of "all of them." I trained myself not to cringe when I would see a crusty older sergeant with a long Special Forces tab on the shoulder of his uniform. Coincidentally, years later in Afghanistan, I would support these units, ride on their convoys, and pass critical intelligence reports to their operators.[31] The Special Forces soldiers I served with down the road were professionals—and understood we were in it together.

Closed doors are just as important as opened doors. I attended other courses, read books, and talked with friends who had "been there, done that." There is so much that can be learned from others; do not overlook this opportunity to grow. I also sought my commission and was promoted to second lieutenant by the end of that year. I had the foundation of two solid years and one combat deployment as an enlisted soldier. And I walked into my new rank as an officer with evidence that supported my father's sage words—a title did not make me a leader. I knew there was still a lot for me to learn.

*In life, people will use names, use words,
to belittle or berate you. You may not
always be taken seriously. There are simply
ugly, angry, and mean people in this world.*

*Do not make sweeping judgments.
Treat each person as a "new day."*

*A person with true fortitude always
takes the higher ground.*

*I'd rather deal with a difficult situation than
a difficult person any day of the week. Yet these
difficult people will be out there—channel
these collisions to fuel your determination.*

★ ★ ★

Arrive Before You Arrive

When you aspire to accomplish something, simply *wanting* to do it isn't enough. First you have to be ready, prepared, *competent,* so when the moment arrives, you succeed. Arrive before you arrive. You have to be competent in order to achieve anything.

What does that mean, though, to be competent? Or as they say in the army, "tactically and technically proficient." It is not as easy as right-clicking on the word and looking at the synonyms, to use one example. It is right-clicking and looking at *all* of the synonyms and being *all* of them: capable, able, knowledgeable, experienced, skilled, proficient, fit, expert, and adept. To be competent, you cannot just be capable. You must also be able. To be competent, you cannot just be knowledgeable. You must also be experienced. Each word means something uniquely different, and all together, they paint the whole picture of what competency really looks like.

I am comfortable with the broad scope of that trait, and in my OIF journal I started the living list of what I needed to focus on to achieve it. First, I identified the goal of becoming an intelligence officer, and ultimately, a commander of a company performing intelligence operations. I saw firsthand during my OIF deployment how intelligence drove operations, and I was hooked. I was also wired for it—I have always wanted to know what is outside of the box that I had perfectly organized and understood. Intelligence professionals need to think like that, in addition to being intensely objective; they must see the world through many lenses.[32] They must resist accepting one answer, or one way to look at things.

Nevertheless, that one goal of becoming "tactically and technically proficient" was threefold; the list I started in my OIF journal would have to cover what would make me competent as an officer, an intelligence professional, and as a commander. There were things that I would have to complete for only one of those roles, but needless to say, all would benefit. Thus I began executing what would make me competent for all of those roles.

Education and attending a variety of army schools would be a cornerstone of this endeavor. I also supplemented my military education with opportunities to study from other institutions and organizations. The main reason I chose to do a masters degree in international security was because it would improve my knowledge as an intelligence officer and the required graduate internship (mine was at the FBI) would broaden my exposure to the intelligence community. In fact, the friendships I made and processes I became aware of turned into critical contacts and sensitive information that helped me deconflict several military operations while I was deployed to Afghanistan later.

I knew what questions to ask, the available resources, and how to better integrate the efforts of other government agencies that were also fighting these wars. Fate would have it that paths cross again. I was fortunate to have dear friends, like Jessica, a fiercely intelligent, hard-charging analyst at the Bureau, or Deb, a strong woman with a beautiful mind and relational prowess from the State Department, both of whom were former graduate school classmates trekking through the same villages more than ten thousand miles away from cozy Denver, Colorado, where we had met a couple years earlier.

In that same vein, I worked as a defense contractor during those years on my road to command, because the defense industry was also providing a disproportionate (enormous!) amount of support for these wars. I needed to understand this part of the puzzle so that I could best leverage their services when I deployed again. Outside of this civilian experience, I also needed to fulfill essential positions within the army to continue to build my platform of competency, and that would include several undesirable positions. For example, commanders will not know how to manage their property books if they have not spent time in the trenches as a company executive officer (XO) whose sole responsibility is just that—managing property. I also made sure to track the obligatory intelligence and staff positions, from S-2 (a unit's intelligence officer) to others that exposed me to a variety of levels so I would understand processes and what affected decision making.

Equally important was the training I received on my road to command—there is no substitute for practicing what you learn. This is also where you need to allow yourself the leeway to make mistakes. And I made plenty. Yet it is in training where you want and need to make mistakes. My old basketball coach was full of powerful mantras, and one of my favorites was, "Practice does not make perfect, only perfect practice makes perfect." This taught me to never cut corners, or be sloppy with my form— practice should be played as if it were the real game. In the army, the same goes: "Train as you fight, fight as you train."

A leader can never prepare too much and, in the same breath, can never be fully prepared.

I prioritized the known areas that were important to my success, from general soldier skills on how to use radios and read maps, to staying in shape and practicing my marksmanship. I found ways to do these things.[33] For instance, I knew that as an officer

I would be issued a pistol. I had grown up shooting rifles, but was not familiar or comfortable with pistols. My husband knew this, and although I joke with him that it was a chance for him to purchase another gun, he gifted me a shiny new M9 Beretta when I was promoted to captain (with my new title engraved on the grips). With the gift came personal lessons from an expert marksman (himself), and before I stepped foot in Afghanistan, I had put more than a thousand rounds through that pistol.

Again, I knew this would be a requirement. There were definitely the unknowns, and things that I could not fully prepare for, like driving in the dark with night vision goggles. You do what you can do, and accept you will not (can not) know everything. Further, you must accept that it all takes time. As the term in the army emphasizes, "Time in grade," which does mean something—it does matter. Yes, sometimes life experiences can make a person wiser and expedite knowledge or maturity. My generation of service members has several of those. But that is not enough by itself to fully prepare and develop that pearl from a grain of sand. It takes time.

And time is what I owed the army. My service obligation was eight years once I received my commission, and the writing on the wall prepared me to expect to be activated again. There were simply not enough service members to fulfill the overextended policy changes and wars of my generation. Not that anyone wanted a godforsaken draft. Still, someone needed to deploy and I was on the books. More importantly, I was prepared and ready to embrace the suck, all over again.

*I had a female commander tell me that she
worked twice as hard as her husband to get
to her rank and position, and that was
because she was a woman. I believed her.*

*It is unfortunate, yet a reality, that
most people will have to work twice as
hard for any number of reasons.*

*Don't look for or dwell on your reason—just work
twice as hard, regardless. You will be better for it.*

PART II: IN COMMAND AND MOBILIZATION

★ ★ ★

Embrace the Suck

"Can you talk?" It was Matt.

"Yeah, just give me a second, I need to step outside." I was sitting with a group of soldiers on a busy drill weekend at Camp Bullis, Texas. By the sound of Matt's voice on the phone, I knew something was going on.

Matt was the assistant operations officer for our battalion. He was a senior captain and tireless workhorse. He was also my former boss. He had recently left the position as commander of Charlie Company, and I had been his company executive officer. We had spent those long, one-weekend-a-month reserve drills working side-by-side, and I soaked up everything he taught me. We had also spent the past couple of years doing the same thing—working full time, going to graduate school full time, and juggling our reserve duties every month. We became good friends through it all. We would schedule our army schools together when it worked out, and we also ended up in Washington DC during the same summer for our graduate school internships (his was at the *other* three-letter agency).

As I walked outside, I realized the last time Matt's voice sounded like that had been on a call a few months earlier, when he told me the battalion was going to receive stop-movement orders. What that meant was our higher command was going to freeze any personnel transfers out of the unit because a warning order would soon follow that would alert the unit to prepare for mobilization. We were slated to go to Afghanistan.

Matt gave me that call that day as a friend and confidant. I remember him saying, "You've already deployed, and you shouldn't have to go on back-to-back deployments with Charles returning home in a few months." You see, Matt gave me that courtesy call because at the time my husband Charles was on an extended fifteen-month tour in Iraq. Matt did the math, and saw that Charles and I would, at best, have a handful of months together once he returned from Iraq, and then I would be shipped out for a year. He added, "Marg, it just doesn't seem fair to you two."

It sure didn't. With that information, I was given a small window of time to transfer and get out of the deployment. When Charles called from Iraq on that night, I had to break the news to him and discuss what we should do. I could hear in his voice that he was crushed. So was I. We not only were counting down the days for his safe return home and finally being together, but also had been privately talking about starting a family as soon as possible. After a heartbreaking conversation, we both knew what our integrity would not permit us to do—it would not be right for me to transfer out of the unit. If my unit was going to be activated, I needed to honor that obligation. I needed to honor the commitment I had to the soldiers with whom I was currently serving. We decided to hold off on our dream of starting a family, and did not tell our loved ones that I was going to deploy until my activation date was clear. With sorrow, we accepted this extremely difficult hand that had been dealt to us. Sometimes you have to embrace the suck.

"Matt, are you still on the line? I'm outside now, and can talk."

"Yes, I'm here. Hey, the new battalion commander (BC) was in my office earlier today and was asking about you. She is hand-selecting her commanders for all four companies, the ones she wants for the deployment, and I'm pretty sure you're on the short list."

I could have jumped up and down with excitement when I heard him say this! Out of all of my ambitions as an officer, becoming a commander was not one that I could just apply for—a command has to be given to you by a BC. It was an honor to be considered, let alone selected. Yet before I could even relish this honor, Matt quickly added, "I know you're not going to like this, but I think she is going to offer you HHC."

"What? Not HHC!" I gasped.

HHC (Headquarters & Headquarters Company) is typically a company an officer would have for his or her second command, and I had yet to have my first! Furthermore, an HHC does not execute the intelligence operations mission—the HHC for my unit would support intelligence operations through various staff functions. I started visualizing Matt blindly being led to this gigantic bear trap as the new BC asked him all the questions that would unearth my potential for an HHC command. "Was Marjorie good with your property book? How was she at coordinating between various levels? What about building morale?" I was silent, mesmerized myself by this new looming trap that was now hanging over my head.

Matt said, "I know you're going to ask, and yes, I did tell her about all the advanced military intelligence training you had, not to mention that you had just completed your master's degree from one of the top ten foreign policy schools. She knows you are prior enlisted, prior deployed, and all the other stuff in your bio . . . Marg, I think she had already made up her mind."

I was in shock. There was another long silence over the phone, and Matt finally said, "I wanted to give you the heads-up so you can think about it before she pitches it to you. Marg, you are going to be a great commander, regardless of what kind of company you lead. Besides, if you say yes, then you can be my boss now."

Matt always found a way to inject humor, in a zany, Happy Gilmore kind of way. I did my best to emulate this quality of his, because an ounce of levity at the perfect moment can work wonders. He was right, as the HHC commander, I would, ironically, be his commander.

With a big sigh, I asked the question for which I already knew his answer. "Matt, what should I do?"

He replied, "That's your call. But you know the old army saying— you are never supposed to turn down a command."

When you are let down, you are simply on the edge of a turnaround.

Disappointment is a part of life, and through those difficult times and decisions, your character will be made.[34] *Your mental and emotional strength will increase.*

And during those disruptive moments, look out for each other—and add some levity, like Matt taught me.

★ ★ ★

Never Turn Down a Command

I had heard that bit of advice before too. If someone above you sees potential in you, embrace it. Rejecting or questioning that vote of confidence can only be interpreted as ungrateful and arrogant. My new BC must have seen something in me that made her come to the decision to offer me the opportunity to lead HHC. She surely did not have lack of other, excellent, options. Perhaps she saw something in me that I did not? I sensed taking on this command was going to feel like falling backwards, giving a perfect stranger blind trust that she would catch me before I hit the ground.

I wrestled with this fate though. At first, I was deflated because I had put so much of my time—my life's direction—into sharpening my knowledge of intelligence operations. Was this all a waste? I had done all that I could, and then some, to be the best candidate, the most competitive choice, for a military intelligence company command. Even the timing to be considered for an opening had worked in my favor. I never even thought to imagine this turn of events. Nevertheless, somewhere along the way the army taught me Moltke's theory of war that "no plan survives first contact."[35] I never planned' on being in the army in the first place, so again, it was time to rely on supple expectations. I should have expected the unexpected with this too.

What I did know for certain was that the current state of HHC was a catastrophe (army lingo would refer to it as a "particular sandwich"). Excluding the handful of active reserve soldiers that kept it afloat outside of those monthly drill weekends, personnel were always coming and going, and never fully manned the roster. It had the lowest morale out of the four companies in the battalion (confirmed by the initial climate survey I gave after I took the command), and the property book was a nightmare. (How do you misplace a Humvee?) Not to mention, you cannot get any closer to the proverbial flagpole—meaning your boss or those in charge. The BC and all the other senior staff were the first "Headquarters" in the HHC—my new boss would have me in her line of sight every day. Being "first in line for the beatings" is the prevailing joke about an HHC command.

Our new BC Monica Harwig had served more than twenty years in the army reserve. She was a seasoned military intelligence officer herself, and had mastered some level of ninja training, because she would spontaneously show up or disappear; those in the room swore she had Harry Potter's invisible cloak. The most memorable thing about her was that she was proudly, unapologetically a Texan. She knew what she believed, and believed what she knew, and much of that was grounded in her Texas heritage. This surely influenced her big vision and high ideals as a leader—Texas size! Second to that, she had that first impression likability factor nailed. Yet, foremost, she was from Texas.

And now *Texas* wanted me to command HHC. For all the wisdom I'd gathered from my first deployment, which included an oath I made to myself to never again "exchange a walk-on part in the war for a lead role in a cage," I was uncertain if I would do exactly that by accepting the HHC command. Time would tell. All I could do was take on the challenge, and be proud that I did not pass up a chance to lead. Besides, it looked like I would have good company in that cage. So when the BC asked me if I would be her HHC commander, I said, "Yes, ma'am."

I then thanked her for the opportunity to lead a company in her battalion, and got to work.

Life does not have detours. You are exactly where you need to be, whether you know it or like it.

One of my soldiers said to me, on one of those first days in Afghanistan, "Ma'am, I've heard that some people choose heaven for the scenery, and hell for the company. By the looks of this place, it's obvious what we chose." He was right.

Help yourself out and just start expecting the unexpected.

★ ★ ★

Perfect Discipline

We all know there is something to first impressions, especially when you are a leader meeting those you are about to lead. One of the prevailing bits of advice about becoming a commander—I heard this from all my army peers and mentors—is to start off strong. When I dug deeper and asked what that meant to them, no two answers were alike. I was told that meant to "drop the hammer" right away on the first infraction, or to "cut the fat" and implement drastic but necessary change. I found that events would dictate exactly how one needs to start off strong. Regardless of the circumstances you face, strength (starting off strong) is grounded in discipline. And discipline needs to start with oneself.

Early on, most soldiers hear the spiel (or should have) that they are now a Soldier, with emphasis on the proper noun status. Every person with whom we come in contact will now scrutinize our individual behaviors. This is why it is beaten into our heads that "we represent something more than ourselves." Even when off duty, how we talk, to how we interact with strangers, will all reflect on how *every* soldier is viewed. Thus soldiers must have self-discipline to carry themselves in the appropriate way—we must always be professional.

Especially as a commander, you are ever more scrutinized and under that microscope.[36] That often-blurred line must be walked, from properly addressing people with titles (which is a show of respect) to being cautious about venting, bad-mouthing, or speaking highly of your "chain of command" (all of which must take into consideration the environment and audience). Even being selective in your associations is important; I can hear my mom now, chiming in, "Birds of a feather flock together." As a commander, I was friendly, but not trying to be a friend— you know the saying, "be a parent, not a peer." Friendships will blossom regardless of circumstances, and that does not have to be at the expense of professionalism. Respect boundaries, yet tear them down with common sense, all through the discretion and self-discipline of striving to be professional.

Once you set and hold the bar for yourself, you can credibly ask that of those you lead.

The first thing a new commander must do is the change of command (COC) inventory—visibly accounting for every piece of equipment and sensitive item on the company's property book. All equipment is then sub-hand receipted to the end user, placing responsibility at the lowest appropriate level. It was early, and my senior NCO and I were covering ground at Camp Mabry, Texas, as he gave me a brisk "lay of the land" before we launched into the dreaded inventory. We walked through more than twenty connexes, a motorpool, training areas, and countless offices that were spread out on this run-down reserve center with its origins in Word War II.

I could, without a doubt, write a separate book about the COC inventory saga—for all *five* that I had to perform for my one company command.[37] This type of inventory is worth millions of dollars, encompassing everything from numerous weapon systems to classified, mission-critical equipment, all shuttled across the country several times and halfway around the world and back (not to mention throughout eastern Afghanistan). It was tiresome, and success relied exactly on the sage advice my drill sergeant had offered years earlier, which I learned later was a quote from General George S. Patton: "You cannot be disciplined in great things and undisciplined in small things. There is only one sort of discipline—perfect discipline."

Since a COC inventory is the first impression a commander can leave on her new company, it is the perfect opportunity to set the tone for General Patton's mantra of perfect discipline—which I translate to mean ruthless consistency and no cutting corners. I painstakingly looked at hundreds, probably thousands, of serial numbers as my new soldiers watched me. I then put the burden of responsibility, in writing, in their hands, and unflinchingly told them if their equipment was misplaced, the expense to replace it would be directly pulled from their next paycheck. I'm certain my economics professors from business school would cheer this practice of aligning incentives to desired behavior.

Soldiers, and, I believe, most people, want to do what is right (be that as rational actors or as predictably irrational actors). A leader needs to provide guidelines, present an opportunity, and insert a little bit of fear that random spot checks of inventory and corrective action can take place at any time.[38] It was during those long first weeks of going through inventory that I stumbled upon what would be one of the most important lessons to impart to my new company—discipline was also a code of behavior I expected them to obey. If one of my top priorities was to take care of them, then one of their top priorities must be the same; they must take care of each other.

Shoved in the back corner of a supply cage were nearly two-dozen army tough boxes and duffel bags filled with personal belongings and individually issued equipment. After piecing the story together from several people, I found out that these boxes and bags belonged to soldiers who had been deployed from our unit (or other reserve units) a couple of years earlier. The soldiers, often referred to as augmentees, had been attached to another unit's battle roster, called up to active duty, and served in either Iraq or Afghanistan. Somehow their boxes and bags had been shipped to Camp Mabry, Texas, and were never returned to them once they returned home.

I was furious! Excuses poured in, from not having enough time on drill weekends to get around to it, to not seeing external markings to identify who it belonged to, or having the funding to mail the gear. The first drill weekend I had my new company in front of me, I cut the locks on a couple of the boxes and dumped them out in front of my soldiers. The majority of them were unaware that this gear had been shelved for years in their reserve center. I told them all that I had learned, and then started sifting through the items, calling out personal belongings, showing family photos, and highlighting the price tag on military gear that the owners of this gear had to pay back to the army—all because they never had their belongings returned to them. Within minutes, nametags and letters gave enough clues to find an identity to attach to the box.

I recall saying, "This is unacceptable. We are soldiers, and we will take care of each other. There is no excuse—you find time, find the money, find the name in the box. You *make* it happen. Fast forward to a year from now, when we are all sitting in Afghanistan together. I want you to think about the things you will bring with you, I want you to imagine that this is your stuff (there may have been an explicative used here). Then, I want you to be able to imagine that the people around you will look out for you and look out for your gear. By the end of today, I want First Sergeant to tell me this is going to be taken care of."

If you are lucky, as I was, you will have a handful of superb NCOs who run with your intent. In very few units in the military do you have the benefit of older, mature soldiers planting themselves, and being a part of that same unit, year after year. Typically, soldiers rotate regularly, so commanders are continually battling turnover. In the army reserve though, you face two extremes; it seems like you are always seeing new faces, and you are always seeing the same old faces.[39] I had soldiers in my company who had been in that unit for more than fifteen years. In fact, many of the soldiers I met in Charlie Company as private first class or specialist would proudly wear the chevrons and ranks of sergeant and staff sergeant under my HHC command.

One of those familiar faces around the battalion was Sergeant Brandi Vineyard. She was one of the NCOs who helped get those long-lost duffels and tough boxes back to their owners—and would perfectly time a well-needed laugh by sharing with me some of the wacky items that had been inventoried. You wouldn't believe what people pack to take with them on a deployment! I did not know Brandi well before I took command of HHC, but by the time I left, she was a trusted confidante and friend. Moreover, she was my consistent reminder that putting people first was a route to mission success.

She was assigned as the battalion's chaplain assistant, and was unassuming and open-minded with everyone she dealt with. Always calm and steady, Brandi's stoic, no-nonsense demeanor was addictive. Furthermore, her fresh (and different) perspective was sheer entertainment value, as it was fun to simply watch her navigate the relatively conservative environment with her unapologetic, I-love-my-NPR liberal views. She would light up when you asked her about her beloved son, who was just a toddler when we deployed. Her commitment to serve in spite of that difficult separation was inspiring.

My company caught on quickly that I was committed to them and the responsibilities of my position, too, through my active engagement and regular presence. "She doesn't let up, does she?" was a comment I overheard in the training area after several drill weekends into my command. No, she doesn't. I took the job seriously, and I had a better idea than most what we were heading into. Starting off strong was the easy *first* step. You must be strong through the middle and to the end. Perfect discipline is consistent, from start to finish.

No one is perfect nor is perfectly disciplined in all things. This is where ruthlessly prioritizing begins. It is up to you to rank those "things."

Make sure that people are first on your list.

Set, hold, and demand high standards. Don't apologize (instead, strive) to be half German Shepherd.

One of those priorities should be that, in some way, you take care of others.

★ ★ ★

Perpetual Optimism

What must also be a constant is a good attitude. There was no better example of this than the man who had the worst job in the company, Sergeant Harry McAllister (Mac), our supply sergeant. Mac was an active guard soldier, holding down the fort full time, often the first to arrive and last to leave. His combat patch was stitched a bit deeper, having earned it during the Gulf War serving on the front lines with a tank unit. He never talked about that experience, but it was evident it had had a significant impact on him. But Mac had somehow found a way for that experience to transform his attitude going forward—in a positive way.

He continued to serve in uniform, and ran circles around himself with the load that was put on his shoulders. Yet every person who had to pleasure of working with him would be met with his kind smile, which was sandwiched between two dark cheeks full of freckles. He was a soft-spoken, pragmatic, get-r-done Tennessee Vols fan who loved his mama and would proudly share photos of his children.

Mac was the first in HHC who got to know me well. We spent more time together than your typical commander–supply sergeant relationship because it was often just us going through inventory. Being in the reserves means you hardly ever have extra hands to help, especially outside of drill weekends. So Mac and I rolled up our sleeves, climbed through connexes, and did the dirty job of looking for serial numbers on outdated equipment side-by-side, sharing stories along the way.

Mac was the first person I had ever met named Harry, which allowed me to share a fun army story. A family member of mine who had been in the army told me before I left for basic training that her drill sergeant always said "Jesus H. Christ" when *excited*. She was told that, clearly, the H stood for Harry (which was suspected to be the first name of that drill sergeant).[40] Mac laughed out loud, and I would learn quickly that he was a good man, deserving of Christ's alleged middle name.

NCOs often pride themselves as "doers," and if ever mistaken in rank for commissioned officers, they will be quick to respond, "I work for a living." Mac saw right away that we were from the same grain of salt; neither of us was afraid of work and both had worked hard our entire lives to get to where we were.[41] That is why I knew immediately it was out of character for Mac to not be the first one at work toward the end of our initial inventory. It was crunch time, and we had several hangnails and a mound of paperwork to wrap up. As I walked through the reserve center, poking my head into different offices thinking Mac might be running in circles somewhere other than his office, I ran into my first sergeant, Top.

"Ma'am, Mac just called. He has chickenpox."

You have got to be kidding me! By the end of the day, Top was the next to confirm that he, too, had the nasty virus. The BC was not happy to extend my inventory deadline, and I received the first of many reproaches from her, because as she said, everything falls back on the commander—I should have gotten it done sooner. As a company commander, you feel the pressure both from those above you and from the most real situation around you (that all of your soldiers are going through). It is imperative to shield your own reprimands and the double layer of burden, and maintain a positive face for your soldiers (as best you can).

Mac and First Sergeant were troopers, and still offered to come in and work. Mac said over the phone, "It's all right, ma'am, it could be worse." Of course he was still upbeat! I thought for sure I was next in line, since I had spent nearly every waking minute with these two over the past month. To top it off, Charles was due to return home from his fifteen-month deployment to Iraq within the next two weeks, and I couldn't help but think he would come home to a wife covered in red dots! But what Mac said rang in my ears. Charles would be home and that was all that mattered.

Surprisingly, I never contracted this terrible virus.

Your attitude (good or bad) is highly contagious, just like chickenpox. Colin Powell said it best: "Perpetual optimism is a force multiplier." This is where my Labrador retriever side barrels through; of course I see the glass half full—what Lab doesn't want to jump in water? As a leader, you find the positive, just like I ordered my soldiers to find a way to get that equipment back to its owners. I made an effort every day to recognize and encourage them. This can be done (and should be done) in front of groups and on a one-to-one basis. Constructive feedback builds confidence and morale, as does including them in my personal objective and having the shared purpose that our company would be exceptional.

I knew just as well as anyone else in the battalion that HHC had issues. Yet that fact never left the confines of my mind once I walked in the door. I walked in like Muhammad Ali—although I was fully aware of the company's shortfalls, I propagated what was being done right and imagined we were the best. My soldiers could believe in this promise; they could believe in me.

The recipe to that credibility started with a belief in both myself, and equally important, in those around me.[42]

*How you respond to crisis influences
how others around you will react.*

*Keep calm and don't apologize (instead, strive)
to be half Labrador retriever
(meaning, look for the positive).*

*And, in order to "float like a butterfly, and sting like
a bee," you must first believe that you have wings.*

Because we all do.

★ ★ ★

Profiles in Courage

The chatter at the reserve center in the early summer of 2009, just six months into my command, was that the battalion could not fill the battle roster. There were simply not enough soldiers who were eligible for deployment because those who had been forced to extend their service obligations under the stop-loss policy were no longer on the hook. Defense Secretary Robert Gates had been true to his word and ordered a deep reduction in how commanders utilized the stop-loss policy, which was the involuntary extension of a service member's military contract, also referred to as the "backdoor draft." This meant that dozens of soldiers throughout the battalion now had a choice: they had to either reenlist to go on the deployment or get out of the army, since their service obligation was complete (or would end during our activation timeframe).

This welcome change to policy couldn't have come at a more inopportune time for my unit; it was instated in August, and we were scheduled to mobilize the following month. Approximately 20 percent of my company battle roster was at risk and I now had to sit down individually with each of these twelve soldiers and explain his or her options. More importantly, I needed to ask them to continue to deploy with the company. I sensed this was just the beginning of difficult conversations I would have with my soldiers as their commander.

With my first sergeant sitting by my side, each soldier was summoned to my office. I explained the change in policy and laid on the table between us the appropriate paperwork. I then brought them into the conversation, listened and asked questions, making it personal that I understood how long they had served already, citing their prior assignments, and so on. Reserve soldiers truly have unique pressures and challenges, juggling a job with all their "weekend warrior" requirements (which takes more of your time than just one weekend a month). They were doctors, police officers, students, and system engineers; men and women; they were someone's children, or had children of their own. Again, my Labrador retriever side makes it natural to empathize, to take interest in their lives and careers.

What I placed on the table next was my request. I did not hold back in sharing the crisis our company was in with this possible shortage of personnel. Each of the positions they individually filled was critical to our mission success, and I explained why. I told them—and meant it—"I need you. The other soldiers in this company need you. You know how the army works; this unit is still going to be sent to Afghanistan, even with the gaps. Maybe we'll get last-minute augmentees. No one really knows at this point. What I do know is that we have a challenging year ahead of us, and I plan to be there for every soldier in our company."

I went on to say, "It is your decision. But you need to know you have my respect for whatever you decide—because you had my respect from the moment you raised your right hand and volunteered to serve in uniform in the first place. Thank you for serving."

These dozen soldiers had to make their decision by the end of the drill weekend. On Sunday night, HHC had retained the largest number of stop-loss soldiers in the battalion. Nine of my soldiers opted to stay in the army and deploy with our unit. They faced fear, putting themselves in personal danger in order to honor a commitment to duty, loyalty, and selfless service, one that they were no longer obligated to make. I thought of their brave act often during our time in Afghanistan. I will always consider those nine soldiers my company's first batch of profiles in courage, and I later gave each of them a copy of that book, *Profiles in Courage*, with a handwritten note of gratitude on the inside cover.

The stop-loss soldiers who continued to serve in my company were people like Sergeant McAllister, resident experts in their specialty and ultimately, a likely single point of failure if they had not deployed because their depth of knowledge and continuity proved to be essential to the company's success in Afghanistan. They were Texans who had been in the unit for years, like Sergeant Lily Becerra, who was one of the best human resource managers in the battalion. They were soldiers who had only recently been assigned to the unit for deployment and didn't know me or anyone else in the company, like Sergeant Drew Dillon from Illinois, a stellar operations analyst. They had rare skills, like Sergeant Eric Burtch, who performed the mission-essential signal intelligence billet, but more importantly at times, kept people laughing with his wit and upbeat perspective. Staff Sergeant Joshua Eldridge also chose to deploy, another soldier with a unique specialization that was a mission-essential skill, yet, more importantly, motivated and coached countless soldiers to peak fitness and health throughout the deployment.

On that Sunday night of drill weekend, the last piece of paperwork I signed was my own stop-loss packet—I never told my soldiers, but I brought the tally up one. I had the choice to stay or go too.

We would go through the next year together, and an inimitable kind of bond would now solidify our connection in life, the way it can when people struggle together. The soldiers in my company would come out stronger and better, as individuals, and as a cohesive unit.

Your current situation in life can be far from ideal, such as being asked to serve in combat when your service obligation is fulfilled, navigating roadblocks to the time you thought you'd start a family, or being offered the "wrong" command when you had your heart (and life's preparation) set on another. Yet, as soldiers, we knew what to do with hardship, what to do with a challenge and the unexpected. We don't run from, we run to the problem, to a solution. *Semper Gumby*, as my marine friends would say. Always flexible. Drive on.

Over the summer, we spent several scorching weeks at Ft. Hunter-Liggett, California, receiving invaluable instruction at the reserve training center (RTC). Another large group of augmentees joined us at RTC, and more would follow as soldiers fell off the battle roster for injuries or a myriad of other reasons. By the time we were mobilized to Ft. Lewis, Washington, in the early fall of 2009, just a little more than nine months into my command, HHC had transformed into a different company. The progress we had made was just in time before we were hit with another unbelievable, unforeseen storm.

*Leadership happens when you
think no one is watching.*

*What do we really have if we don't have each other?
We can do this—together.*

The hard choice is often the right one.

Be a person others can count on.

$$\star \quad \star \quad \star$$

There Is No Bench Team

"Matt, we've got to talk."

Barreling into the S-3 shop, I was desperate to share the game-changing, unexpected update I had just received on our classified email system.

It was September, and we were a few weeks into our final pre-deployment training at Ft. Lewis. Our deployment date was set for October, in which we would be loading up to head over to Afghanistan.

"Hey, I needed to talk with you too. The BC wants to know if you picked HHC's company team name—you're the last to submit this to her and she's not happy."

Yeah, I thought, I'm the last because I didn't just sit with my first sergeant and come up with it on my own (like the other companies). I sent it out to every soldier in my command to have a say, and for him or her to make recommendations on our name. Just because we're in the military doesn't mean we can't have a democratic process every now and then—especially when it makes sense and I need their buy-in.

Nevertheless, I had bigger problems at that time.

"Well, my company name is the last thing on my mind right now.

I just received a message from George [my counterpart currently in Afghanistan who I was set to replace], and he said the organizational charts are all wrong."

Matt took a moment to review the documents I handed him, and his upbeat, zany demeanor started to immediately drain from his body. I stood there quietly, wishing I didn't have to deliver this news, especially since I knew Matt must have been working twice as hard to maintain a good attitude. He had recently returned from a quick trip home to be with his wife as she gave birth to their first child. I couldn't imagine the weight on his shoulders, knowing he would spend the first year of that baby's life away from her.

After a few minutes, Matt looked up, "This will change everything. I've got to make a few calls."

"I understand. I'm going to check in with the one shop [army lingo for personnel office] to see if my lieutenant arrived yet, and I'll swing back through."

Matt was dialing numbers on his phone before I even walked out of his office. As I headed over to the personnel office, I shook my head and felt like a fool: I'd thought the last soldier to fill my current battle roster of approximately fifty—and my biggest problem—was supposed to be this brand new lieutenant set to arrive any day. That *had* been my biggest battle at the time, fighting for a more seasoned officer to fill my company executive officer (XO) position, since the person who held that job would manage the largest property book in the battalion, with the most moving parts. Despite the extra time it took for me to train Lieutenant Tara Briggs when she reported for duty (over the first few weeks in a combat deployment, mind you), I was reminded you want someone with a good attitude and strong work ethic (like hers) over a few years of additional experience.

But now, with the new information from downrange, it looked like my company was about to explode—George had told me he was in charge of an element that included a typical HHC *and* a military intelligence collection mission. In short, it was two companies rolled into one, and the intelligence mission covered the full spectrum of operation specialists: interrogators, counter-intelligence agents, signal collectors, and an unattended ground sensor team. Good news: it was what I had been preparing myself to lead for years. Bad news: in less than four weeks, I had to build approximately a dozen intelligence teams that would be spread out over three provinces, on half a dozen forward operation bases, in my area of operations in eastern Afghanistan. My company would more than double in size and equipment.

Only one part of this major battalion realignment was relatively painless and that was moving the largest signal collection team under my authority. This team was referred to by the name of their operation, the ROCC (Remote Operations Cryptologic Center). These nearly twenty ROCC soldiers now under my command were tasked with providing signal analysis support and training to International Security Assistance Forces for *all* of Afghanistan. What this meant was I was inheriting some of the smartest, mission critical, most interesting problem solvers that serve in the United States Army—and they were led by one of the absolute best in the field.

Captain Steven Starkey, the officer in charge of the team, was also, like many of its members, a new augmentee to the unit. Although he was a native Texan, he was activated from a civilian job that had him working in Germany (and quite rooted: affianced to a fun German woman, gearing up to start a family). I couldn't be happier to work with him since we had already begun to strike up a friendship those first few weeks of our pre-mobilization training. Steven was impeccably witty, happy-go-lucky, earnest, and kind. He ran like the wind, had an incredible aptitude to relate with others, and a quirky likability factor that was off the charts. He instantly became my confidant and friend.

It was a tremendous relief to have Steven at the helm of the ROCC so I could place my attention on building the other teams in my new company. This was where I needed to be, because it had become the nightmare before the dream. Once the other company commanders learned they would be required to restructure their units and transfer a certain number of soldiers (by job specialty) to HHC, the jockeying began. For a period of three weeks, the battalion faced constant uncertainty, which was tremendously disruptive because soldiers were being moved around daily to fill different teams on different company battle rosters. The upside to these ridiculous battle roster changes was that soldiers got to know each other throughout the battalion—they would literally stand in one company's formation in the morning, then another by afternoon—although it was a minor benefit in comparison.

At first, the other commanders passed along most of the new augmentees because they didn't know these soldiers. That is when names I had never heard before populated my battle roster, from specialist to staff sergeants, like Tes Shabazz, Joel Lundy, Sam Durham, and Brad Schmidt. As one would expect, the other commanders fought to keep those who had been training with their companies the longest since they had already been vetted. Yet the rationale to dump all the new guys into HHC was dangerous—on an individual level and for team building. Besides, I didn't want my new intelligence company to feel like they had been thrown away. I had to plead with Texas that common sense and risk mitigation had to be taken into account.

After several late nights of bartering and negotiations, the army maxim that *we can either succeed or fail together* prevailed. For instance, my area of operation included the French-owned battle space; therefore, practical collaboration resulted in all the French linguists to transfer to my command regardless of simply being locked into a prior company because that's where they had always been assigned (like Lauren Taylor and Pierre Lambert). My peer, Charlie Company Commander Chris Figueroa (Fig) was the most decent and logical throughout this ordeal. Fig knew I had several strong bonds with soldiers in his company because I had spent a couple of years there (before him) as a lieutenant. This was when I became reunited with a few familiar faces, like Rick Groff, Mark Harritt, Jesse Miller, John Greenfield, and Kristy James. This was a tremendous morale boost for me. It is reassuring to feel like you know a person when you go to battle together. And we had already made a connection: from time laughing in the barracks during field training to knowing the personal stories, like Groff being a proud father of two and Harritt being the proud son of a women who served in the US Women's Army Auxiliary Corps in World War II.

With only a couple of weeks to spare, my new company was beginning to take form. It was an impressive mix of legacy 321st soldiers to new soldiers who were activated from all across the country (and I mean, from Hawaii to Maryland, and yes, even Starkey from Germany). At the end of the day, we had every walk of life, from soldiers like Sergeant Kelly Hoffman who actually was in the military just after the Vietnam War and has a son who was wounded serving in Iraq, to several who were turning around to serve back-to-back tours like Sergeant First Class David Lopez. And for a bunch of weekend warriors as the US Army Reserve is often described, we were clearly no bench team. Every soldier brought invaluable civilian careers, knowledge, and perspective, not to mention several brought numerous (and multiple) prior combat tours to the fight in Afghanistan.

Now I had a very short window to ensure they knew this before they would spread to the wind on several bases in Afghanistan. Reaffirming their worth and communicating my belief in them was nothing like the first Muhammad Ali iteration I'd had to duck and jab through months earlier. This time, perpetual optimism resonated from several of my original HHC soldiers—most notably Mac. While onboarding a new transfer, I overheard him say, "Welcome to the best company in the battalion." All over again, I started to see my soldiers live up to the high expectations I held for them. We were, we would be, the best company in the battalion.

And we had an appropriate name that helped us live up to that legacy. Now well into October, while I was packing a bag for the unit's last weekend pass before we were set to fly overseas, Starkey and his NCOIC, Sergeant First Class Mark Harritt, walked into my makeshift office with two sloppy smiles on their faces that could only say, "I know something that you don't know." I smiled back and said, "All right guys, what's going on?" Like peas in a pod, they took turns chiming in, interlacing gravity and humor when delivering the message: "Ma'am, the soldiers of HHC have selected their name."

Since our task force was called Dark Knight, the company teams had to follow this medieval theme and choose a name accordingly. This was annoying because I would have preferred getting away from the "crusader" misnomer. I had no idea what to expect, but I never expected what Starkey and Harritt shared: "With the final vote tallied tonight, we are here forth now known as Company Team Longbow. We are *the* weapon made from a single piece of wood, that history can attest changed the course of many wars. For centuries, we were known as the battlefield weapon of choice, with undeniable impact and with the ability to have the furthest reach. And by the way, with you as our commander standing at six feet tall, you're perfectly suited to take us into combat and prosper."

I now know why they walked into my office with those smiles. I couldn't get the same smile off of my face. I wanted to laugh out loud, jump for joy, and cry out that *that* name was perfect!

The wild ride of our pre-mobilization time sank in hard and deep on those last few quiet nights at Ft. Lewis. On a rainy overcast weekend while the entire battalion was on pass, tucked away at a bed-and-breakfast on Bainbridge Island, I shared with Charles the final name (and sing-song definition) for my company. He, too, laughed out loud and smiled. "I love it," he said. Privately, I felt stronger and closer to him with that company name, too; after all, he had spent years as an Apache *Longbow* helicopter pilot, fifteen months of that time flying in combat. And he had just returned home from that tour a few months before.

It was now time, again, to say good-bye. Regardless, he was with me, because so many of my better qualities as a soldier and as a leader were directly a result of his influence. For the record, saying good-bye when deploying to combat never gets easier— despite how many times we had to do this.

What I arrived with, and what I was leaving with, and all that work in between to build teams from strangers—to mission ready— was absolutely unexpected and unprecedented. That challenge alone already felt like I'd been through hell, but I knew better than that. As Sergeant Harritt would say on one of those first few days in Afghanistan, looking beyond the perimeter of our base, "It may feel like it, but we are not in hell yet. I can see it from here, though."

In service, there is no bench team.
Everyone is immediately in the game.[43]

You may not get to choose your team, but at the end
of the day it's about your team choosing you.

Face every day, every situation, with unyielding
conviction and supple expectations—in that order.

It doesn't matter if you believe in a mission if you
don't believe in the people who make it happen. Ask
for input from the people making it a realization.

(clockwise, from top left)   1. *This photo is from my Basic Training -*
     Advanced Individual Training days (2002).

2. *Sitting on the tailgate of a Chinook helicopter,*
   flying over "Mesopatamia" in 2003.

3. *Meeting with village leaders at a local orphanage in*
   Bamyan, Afghanistan (2010).

(from top) 1. *Corporal Lauren Taylor on a village patrol in Eastern Afghanistan (2010).*

2. *SSG Joshua Eldridge passing out the cold weather clothes his church provided to the Bamyan, Afghanistan orphanage (2010).*

(from top)   *1. Reenlisting Specialist Pitts on the flight line at Bagram Airfield (2009).*

2. Corporals Nick Corder and Carly Andersen passing out Claire's Denver Beanie Babies in Bamyan, Afghanistan (2010).

Taking the company guidon on another mission. We were just about to convoy the MRAP behind us and deliver it to the team in Kapisa Province (2009), with: Corporal Joel Lundy, Sergeant Alex Kimball, Staff Sergeant Brad Schmidt, and Sergeant Marco Vasquez.

Company Team Longbow's Combat Patch Ceremony (2009), and faces you can see (L-R: me, Flook, Lynette, Hoffman, Gempler, Vineyard, Becerra, Winston).

The front door of my command post after the team personalized it with arrows pointing in the direction of where they wanted to be.

The MRAP in the foreground was the truck Sergeant Jesse Miller and I were in when we drove over the IED. The culvert is behind us, with the robots employed and close air support overhead.

You can tell how much fun these guys had together. (L–R): Skip, Staff Sergeant Rick Groff, and one of the French soldiers from their FOB.

Rashid and Corporal Ashley Johnson standing on the edge of a cleared minefield, next to the largest weapons cache recovery outside Bagram in 2010.

(clockwise, from top left)

1. *Captain Steven Starkey posing in front of the live Douglas fir that Charles shipped to the company as a Christmas gift in 2009.*

2. *Staff Sergeant Harry "Mac" McAllister working the property books, taking care of soldiers.*

3. *Final Company Team Longbow board, with unit patches identifying who we were with and supported in Eastern Afghanistan 2009–2010.*

(from top)

1. Lieutenant Tara Briggs and Sergeant Brandi Vineyard celebrating the delivery of a new mattress they snuck in my room (note the Christmas lights in the background), 2010.

2. The day after Henk's surgery and the day we learned he had cancer (2012).

3. Henk as a little boy, cancer-free (2015).

4. My last photo in uniform, sitting next to the best soldier I ever served with, Charles (2011).

PART 3: AFGHANISTAN

★ ★ ★

You See a Light, You Don't Hear One

"Did you hear that?" Top asked.

"Hear what?" I replied.

No sooner did I speak than the sound of rockets crashing in the distance became very clear. *Boom. Boom. Boom.*

"I heard that. Don't even wait for the siren, Top, start 100 percent accountability alert now."

Every service member remembers the first time they heard rocket attacks, the different sound of a bullet being shot toward them, or the thunderous explosion caused by close air support responding to their TIC (troops in contact). I sure do. What you would also remember if you lived at Bagram for more than a day was the constant din of various obnoxious noises. It didn't help that I lived alongside the airfield in a plywood box (called a CHU—a containerized housing unit) that eventually got a few rows of sandbags piled around the outside to help contain any blasts from unwelcome rockets. More annoying than the constant noise of aircraft and the full afterburner takeoffs of F-15 jets climbing into the sky like homesick angels were the hundreds of *birds* that never shut up!

Oh, how I yearned for peace and quiet. Even at night, especially at night, flocks of birds would chirp—nonstop—and crowd the lines strung between looming stadium lights near the perimeter. During my first few weeks at Bagram when I was walking by those lights that turned night into day, I realized—amongst the cacophony chorus of confused birds—that even the lights made a zipping hum. I couldn't help but shake my head and laugh. Instantly, I was reminded of one of my favorite sayings that I had learned from a youth pastor: "You see a light, you don't hear one." *So much for that*, I thought. That youth pastor had not been to Bagram.

Nonetheless, the concept still meant something to me, as it was not only a spiritual beacon for my life but it also inspired my command philosophy. A command philosophy is yet another impressive army term that describes how an organization will operate. Military culture has long extolled the tradition of new commanders outlining standards (high but realistic, with easily understood guidelines) for their troops to follow. The philosophy can be posted on company websites and in common areas, or read out loud at the change of command ceremony, during which most soldiers are focusing more on not locking their knees and passing out than actually listening. The truth is, though, hardly anyone reads these or hears them read out loud, let alone internalizes their greater meaning. Albeit a necessary practice to put on paper (as we all know the value of having a map), soldiers understand a unit's vision, goals, and objectives best by observing the attitude, behaviors, and actions of the person in charge.

We've all heard the saying, "Actions speak louder than words." They do.

At a relatively young age, I went through an extreme situation that tested my ability to lead men and women, no less—in combat. As a company commander, I was at the action level where the MRAP met the road. I believe that it was due to actions (not merely words) that resulted in my company's remarkable performance.

I want to share what I have learned thus far about leadership: there are not five *traits*, or one *style*, or *the book* that uncovered *the secret* to being an outstanding leader. Trust me, I think I read them all (or tried to) before I was appointed a commander. The holy grail I unearthed (as others have before me) is this: there is no leadership guide that is one-size-fits-all. This is why there are many excellent leaders but none who are exactly alike.

Great leaders can be introverts or extroverts, tall or short, male or female. Time-tested examples illustrate some of the top qualities of successful leaders as those who listen; who care about their subordinates; who are competent, trustworthy, and trusting; who are authentic and ace the exam on character. The living list of what makes an effective leader is both obvious and intricate. Nevertheless, your behaviors, actions, and attitude determine how you implement such leadership values and beliefs; they are *how* a leader is heard and are what must be *seen* by those who are led.

Soldiers *saw* Captain Starkey show up on time for everything, which was a sign of respect for others. My unit *saw* battalion leadership make time for physical training, which set an example of personal fitness and accountability for everyone (as Texas said, if the president can make time to exercise, so can I; or, she'd state simply, it's the right thing to do). And when soldiers throughout the battalion checked in with Sergeant Mac, whether for inventory or advice, he always heard them out and met them where they were. In all environments, and lived daily, great leaders incite the values that positively affect an organization's moral and operational compass.[44]

In the same way, a toxic leader can influence an organization too.[45] In fact, we often learn about leadership through examples of what not to do. Recall the humorous adage, "Do as I say, not as I do." In the army, for instance, more than one bad officer or senior NCO evoked the derogative expression, "Rank has privileges." But the only privilege a leader should take is the honor to serve, enable, and inspire those beneath (and around) them. A few examples of how this translates to actions in the army are: bunk in the same quarters as your soldiers; never have to qualify twice on your weapon (like those who will not be named); clean your own rifle; carry your own bags; and take your physical fitness test with your subordinates (and in front of them). Soldiers understand the common sense exceptions that are required for certain positions and, moreover, recognize the abuses.[46]

Leaders are always under the microscope—in everything they do, they are setting an example. "Lead from the front" is a long-standing army maxim that means that as a leader, you go before anyone else, you show the way by example in thought, word, and deed—yet, you should always be the last one to eat.[47] This motto is not only meant in an operational sense but, more importantly, in upholding ethical standards. Said bluntly, leaders should not be sexually unrestrained, they should not run shady deals, bad-mouth others (critical, not criticize), or circumvent regulations.

This is not to say that people want a perfect boss or a perfect leader—that is unreasonable. We are all human, and we all make mistakes. Yet there is a lot to be said for genuinely trying to do what is right through your actions and behaviors; an honest effort means something. We must try to glean a little knowledge from everywhere and everyone, good and bad, subordinates, peers, and superiors alike. The lessons I learned from Sergeant Vasquez about trust (demonstrated in the diligence he placed in being a convoy leader) were equally as prescient as seeing General Stanley McChrystal just show up throughout the battle space, from dropping in to check in with one of our battalion collection teams to talking with my class, which was packed with Coalition and Afghan Army soldiers at the Kabul Counterinsurgency Leadership Course.

Furthermore, we collect our personal wisdom on leadership through every position, through every chapter in our lives. At any one point during my ten years of post 9/11 military service, I would have offered a different emphasis or perspective on leadership because I have grown through the numerous crucibles in my life. We know that significant events shape people, but they undeniably shape leaders, too, who emerge stronger. Author Harry C. Garner describes it best in his article "Developing an Effective Command Philosophy":

> *Crucibles are transformational events. Through crucibles, an individual gains a new or altered sense of identity. These life-altering events might include combat, life-threatening disease, the death of a spouse or child, or a professional or financial crisis such as job loss or bankruptcy. They may also include positive events such as marriage, the birth of a child, or a promotion. Maybe simply growing up on a farm in central Iowa engrained the values of hard work, dedication, and faith into your consciousness. Whatever the crucible, explore and reflect upon your own personal values, assumptions, and beliefs about leadership [codify the changes that result].[48]*

My leadership journey in the military helped me mature. When I was a lower-ranked enlisted soldier, I acquired increased sensitivity to what it feels like to be a subordinate (especially while deployed to combat). Through numerous jobs in the civilian sector, and advanced staff positions in the army, I became more attuned to "all the moving parts" (of an operation), a phrase my first sergeant often used. Through it all, I was molded by the countless examples I observed, and learned how others—of all ranks—led around me. Leadership must evolve, and my time in Afghanistan presents the accumulation—it offers all that I had absorbed up to that point.

Although leadership will (must) evolve, I noticed during my ten years of military service that there was always one aspect that remained the same, at every level, through every crucible. Just as we know that leadership comes to its fullness in troubling times, a person's attitude, behaviors, and actions are the consistent, prevailing factor that transmits his or her leadership principles—good or bad.

What naturally unearths itself are those deep, inner qualities that we must develop and channel. With that, I am an advocate of a strength-based approach to life and leadership.[49] I believe what author Tom Rath presented in his book, *Strengths Finders 2.0*, "that each person has greater potential for success in specific areas, and the key to human development [and leadership] is building on who you already are." Be aware of your weaknesses, but put more of your energy into improving your talents.[50] Your best is grounded in your strengths. Know yourself, and then make sure you are not surrounding yourself with groupthink. Diversity (in every way) should be treated like a verb (think cognitive and strength diversity).

Furthermore, a person's moral foundation may also bind or blind a person's attitude, behaviors, and actions. Studies have shown that we are born with ethical instincts, and we often feel and show these ethics before we rationalize our decision on why we do what we do.[51] Again, we must be self-aware, and channel the best of who we are when we are leaders.

Because the truth is, we are all leaders to someone, at all times. Someone is watching our actions and is influenced by our attitude and behaviors this very moment. This is all the more reason we should choose to *be a light*. Leadership, after all, is a choice.

JOURNAL ENTRY FOR 23 NOVEMBER 2009

"So help me God"

The MRAP for HCT19 [human intelligence collection team] was delivered today, and I got my first ride in that huge monstrosity, across BAF to my command post (CP). Like nearly all of my soldiers, the first time they will most likely ride in these behemoths will be here, in Afghanistan, along IED-laden roads. Best part about my morning was reenlisting one of my soldiers, Specialist Pitts. I thankfully refreshed my memory of the oath during long, drawn-out meetings.) My soldier needed to know that I value the oath I was giving him, to know its gravity, and one way that is shown is by my reciting it from memory. *"I (state your name), do solemnly swear, to support and defend the Constitution of the United States, against all enemies, foreign and domestic, and bear true faith and allegiance to the same. I will obey the orders of the President of the United States and of those of the Officers appointed over me, according to Regulations and Uniform Code of Military Justice. So help me God."*

Pitts asked if we could do his reenlistment on the flight line, in front of an F-15. Of course, I said (thinking of how loud that will be . . . apparently he doesn't mind their noise!). The fighter pilots were good sports and happy to oblige . . . their demeanor reminded me of Charles. Hell, someone could "fly a desk" right now, and they'd make me think of Charles. Tonight, walking to the gym for a quick workout, I realized those stadium lights with all the damn birds on them even make a noise!

Well, if I can't find peace and quiet here, I think I have found the only place in all of Afghanistan where I actually can zone out and have time to myself—and that is running on the treadmill. Lord knows I'm constantly bombarded everywhere else, even in the showers or bathroom stalls, people want to talk or ask questions. Yuck. On the treadmill, I can put my ear buds in, and no one interrupts. The only thing that interrupted my AC/DC playlist tonight was the sound of the Lt. Dan Band, playing a USO concert in the clamshell tent next to the gym. That didn't bother me though. I popped my head in after my run and saw Gary Sinise rocking out on a guitar. Very strange, Forrest Gumpy-kind of funny seeing him over here, in this place . . . thank God someone from back home hasn't forgotten about us. I swear it feels like I am on Mars. I received a care package from home (Earth), and it was a nice reminder of "the warmth of days gone by . . ."

JOURNAL ENTRY FOR 05 FEBRUARY 2010

"I walk the line"

You have to draw the line too. And that was what today was about for one of my soldiers. He repeatedly said he was sorry when he had the chance to speak this morning during his counseling. I had no choice other than to reduce him in rank for his "lack of judgment." Some situations, such as drunk driving or domestic violence, violate the soldier's expected code of behavior in a way that does not allow a commander to be flexible with the punishment. A precedent must be set, and this young soldier is smart enough to know what he did was inexcusable. He will course correct, I'm certain. This one is a good soldier, just in a bad place in his life.

I try to take every situation and adjust my approach for maximum effect. (Sometimes that requires more compassion than punch, or vice versa.) What every disciplinary counseling has in common is I stress (as I did today) that the soldier needs to take responsibility for his or her actions, learn from them, and move forward. Forward, it is.

All I could do was be pulled forward throughout the day, as I was swamped after this morning's counseling. Too many meetings . . . I finished the monthly report on UGS tonight, and the tally for our first operational month equated to thirty soldiers trained, on three FOBs (Tangi, Metharlam, Kalagush), with three different units, in two areas of operations. Throw on top of that three BAF command briefs, a new portal site to streamline requests . . . What a launch, and it has been so much due to the fact that I have two technically savvy airmen rowing this boat. Sergeant Justin Baker has especially shined, as he has a knack for the technical requirements. He is such an impressive young man, always smiling. Service members are resilient, resourceful, and no two are alike! That's the value of diversity—so many different strengths, combined they get the job done.

JOURNAL ENTRY FOR 25 JULY 2010

"Have one of the lower enlisted soldiers clean the colonel's M4"

That's what she told Harritt today. He was outright disgusted, and did not follow her orders. He lamented to Starkey, his platoon leader (and friend), and they took care of it. There was no way in hell (or Afghanistan) any of us would have allowed that to happen. Starkey sat in my office tonight, after a very long day, and cleaned the colonel's rifle. The colonel probably doesn't even know. Turns out this same person ordered a different soldier to clean her rifle too. Errr!

We only found out about that after the fact, so we couldn't subvert the entitled laziness. Brandi told me about this at dinner. She has her thumb on the pulse and is always attuned to the happenings in this unit. Her emotional quotient far exceeds that of a normal person, as does her willingness to be out front with the troops. I am going to miss our daily friendship and being inspired by her grit. I can't think about that now . . .

How you lead your own life will have more impact on others than any command philosophy you may one day espouse.

Therefore, be a light. Not a Bagram light . . . just a light.

And leave the light on—all of the time.

★ ★ ★

Sometimes You Should Cry

"Ma'am, do you want to walk together down to Battalion? The chaplain is already there, waiting for us." Brandi had popped her head into my command post to ask, probably more so to remind me, that I had to start moving in that direction. I was happy to see her, but not thrilled to stop what I had been working on. I had no choice though. Thankfully, when you're tired and cranky, a friendly face helps.

We were all tired and a little bit (some more than others) irritable. We had only been in Afghanistan for two weeks, which meant each and every soldier was doubled up with the unit we were replacing, our counterparts. The army calls this a relief in place (RIP), in which the unit that has been deployed sits in the left seat "driving," while the replacement unit (which was us at this time) sits in the right seat drinking from a fire hose. You have to learn as much as you can in those few short days from people who are *over* their deployment and just want to go home. On the flip side, you are on the front of the deployment—sleep-deprived from traveling, in shock from stepping into hell, adjusting to the new environment, and separated from loved ones. Not to mention a bit unnerved from those first booms landing on the base at any hour of the day.

Then, what feels like unnecessary requirements (some are), all seem to pile on top. That was exactly what I was feeling about heading to Battalion that moment—it was ridiculous! Brandi and I needed to meet up with the chaplain so we could go through the steps of a "practice memorial ceremony." It was on our RIP checklist of things we needed to do, and I was the unlucky company commander who had to fill in and learn the process for the battalion with our chaplain team.

I was annoyed, to say the least, because I had several teams pushing out to various forward operations bases. There were reports I needed to read and equipment (like MRAPs) I needed to order so they had the best. My time could be used in such a better way, I thought. My resistance was not rooted in the fact that going through the motions for something like this is sickening. I can get through uncomfortable—I'm in the army, in a combat zone, after all. And it was not for the fact I didn't think we would need to know how to do one of these ceremonies. The odds said we did.[52]

Needless to say, I'm not the person who took time to write that "last letter." Like my father, people know what I think of them within five minutes, and if anything changes, I tell them. Or, my Irish-German eyes give me away. I get it, some gain value from these things. However, I just wanted and needed to spend my time doing everything I could so that I would *not* have to attend a real memorial ceremony. I learned too quickly, that's not necessarily in our hands.

JOURNAL ENTRY FOR 11 NOVEMBER 2009

"Incoming"

What a Veteran's Day, for the books. Started off the day by delivering a Red Cross message to one of my soldiers who lost an elderly family member back home. The soldier had just gone to bed after working the night shift, so his team leader (Starkey) and I had to wake him. He immediately broke down and started to cry. As much as I strive to carry myself in uniform as the "non-huggy, non-touchy female-type," I knew instantly that it didn't matter how girlie I would be perceived. That soldier needed a shoulder to cry on, and by instinct, I immediately grabbed and held on. Showing compassion is not a sign of weakness, and it is not being girlie. It is leadership, and that reminder hit me in the gut today. And it reminded me of a feeling from my last deployment, when I hugged my tent-mate, Mary. We were going on to different locations from our original FOB and it dawned on me then that I had gone months without hugging or being hugged. That is such a strange feeling.

I did my best to console my soldier, and Starkey took it from there. He is such a great officer, and I am so lucky he is in my company. Next, one of my collection teams based out of BAF received a tip from a local national that led them to a weapons cache outside the gates. It was such a rush to coordinate the elements so that my guys could do their job. After a controlled detonation, several rockets were destroyed and can no longer get into the wrong hands.

Just as I was capturing all this in my battle update brief (BUB) for the next morning, we received incoming rockets from those "wrong hands." Four loud blasts on the opposite side of the airstrip, damaging connexes and equipment—but no people were injured. We did our 100 percent accountability, and it went smoothly. Every soldier who checked in had a new look on his or her face. This was all suddenly, very, very real. So that was my day, my day as a veteran, on Veteran's Day, in a combat zone, experiencing rocket attacks from Taliban fighters.

JOURNAL ENTRY FOR 12 NOVEMBER 2009

"Round Two"

Rocket attacks again tonight. And again, all of my soldiers are safe and accounted for . . . another crazy day, busy, directing, motivating, organizing, go, go, go . . .

JOURNAL ENTRY FOR 13 NOVEMBER 2009

"KIA – Specialist Coffland"

Today is a day I had hoped and prayed I would never experience—we lost a soldier today from our unit. SPC Christopher Coffland was a cross-level augmentee from the 323rd, was in a few different companies through our train-up, and finally landed in Alpha Company. He was killed by an IED this morning—and he was in an MRAP! When I learned from the battle captain just before lunch (he called my secure phone line at my desk) that we had to go "blackout" because of a KIA (killed in action), I knew from the sound of his voice this was not a drill (because we are still in the RIP process, "rehearsing").

My heart changed in that moment and I sense it will never be as it was before. My S-6 shut down all Internet access (foremost, so that no one would alert his family back home before the army could). I immediately pulled in Top and Tara (my XO), and told them the news. Like a switch, I immediately started a list of things to do, from prioritizing contact with the NCOs who knew him well, to alerting all of the team leaders. As much information as quickly as possible had to get out to the company.

One of my team leaders in particular—Rick Groff—was his good friend. I called his office first since he was on a different FOB, asked for the assistant team leader (Greenfield), and told him that I needed both him and Rick to call me back immediately, by themselves. I wanted to make sure Rick had someone with him, but also needed to clear the room so no one else would hear us on speakerphone. I remained calm and strong, and told them all that I knew. It broke my heart to hear the silence on the other end of the phone.

Only because I have all of my soldiers looking at me, and know that they need to see calm and strong, can I do this. On the inside, I am weeping. I was able to cry with George tonight [my counterpart with the 636th MI Battalion that we are replacing]. He wept with me. He barely got all of his soldiers out of this place in one piece (with several Purple Hearts). And, I could tell he knew what he was leaving better than I knew what I was stepping into.

I have consoled, hugged, informed . . . all day. I am empty.

I didn't know Coffland well, but I knew of him well enough to enjoy his antics. He always had a broad smile on his face and became infamous when he spelled out his name at a barbeque during our train-up at Ft. Hunter-Liggett. That was the same night I recall meeting him, as he served extra glasses of wine to me. When I went to hand him my two tickets (which was the limit), he leaned in, mischievously smiled and said, "Just keep those tickets and come back for more!" I was in a PT [physical training] uniform, so he didn't know that I was a commander. I smiled back and knew it was harmless. When he saw me the next day, in uniform, he was surprised.

Sharing these light moments was necessary tonight, too, when I had my company in front of me. Others pitched in with great stories, and it was very clear that we all knew why we needed to stay focused, and keep moving forward—it was now for Coffland. My soldiers are shaken, mortified, as we've only been here for two and a half weeks. God, please be with Coffland's family when they find out tonight. My heart aches for them. Please be with all of my soldiers, bring them peace and strength. Please be with me, so that I am strong for my company. I wish I could talk with Charles right now. This is horrible. I must try to get some rest—I will only have two hours of sleep tonight because the ramp ceremony will be at sunrise, in which his flag-laden coffin will be carried onto a plane for his final flight home. I hate war. Tonight, I hate the Taliban more.

JOURNAL ENTRY FOR 14 NOVEMBER 2009

"My country 'tis of thee, sweet land of liberty . . ."

An army band played this song this morning—on horns—which made it uniquely sad and moving. It was played on the tarmac, on an airstrip here at Bagram Airfield, for a ramp ceremony. A ramp ceremony is the most heart-wrenching ceremony to experience. I quietly sobbed along with everyone else, while standing in formation, at attention, rendering my right arm in a four-second delayed salute, while my soldiers carried the flag-draped coffin with SPC Coffland's remains.

We were outside, in the brisk early morning, paying our last respects to a soldier who lost his life fighting this damn war, these damn monsters, who cowardly bury bombs alongside of roads. The ceremony will forever be seared into my memory. Several of my soldiers knew Coffland well, and I have them on light duty. Nothing more can really be said other than rest in peace, dear soldier. Godspeed on your flight home . . . Dear God, I pray that I never have to attend one of these ceremonies again. I pray.

JOURNAL ENTRY FOR 18 NOVEMBER 2009

"The dash between"

Today was another rough day, from being nitpicked at the morning BUB on my company operations to sidestepping all the tension from staff. Nerves are frayed. I see what Captain Bettinger had to go through today, being the commanding officer reading a eulogy about one of his lost soldiers . . . I felt incredibly sad for him. We all need to remember this moment, what matters, and my hope is that some will stop "creating" drama. The chaplain gave an amazing benediction today at SPC Coffland's memorial (it felt like a year ago that we practiced this, although it had only been days). He read a poem about "the dash between," which is between the year you are born and the year you die. What matters is that dash—what you do with your life, if you are living to the fullest, and what you put into it. People remember the dash.

I have tried to live my life with enthusiasm, love, and focus . . . I will now live and love a little bit more for Coffland, and stay motivated to do my job well, and buck the bullshit. God, I believe you wouldn't put me through anything I wasn't equipped to handle. I believe You touched my heart to set my own dreams aside of starting a family with Charles this year, so that I could go on this deployment, with these

soldiers, this family. I trust You will continue to guide me.
I pray tonight that You protect them.

*Sometimes crying is just how
your mind and heart talk.*

*Leaders must be open, honest in
all ways, and vulnerable.*

*"What matters is how we live and
love and how we spend our dash."*[53]

*We've disconnected the consequences
of war from the American public when
less than 1 percent serve. We must all know,
and never forget, our nation's heroes.*

$\star$ $\star$ $\star$

Christmas Lights All Year

"Can someone please tell me why in the hell this big-ass box is still cluttering the entryway to the CP?"

It was early in the morning, and I was standing in the front part of my company's command post (CP), staring at a box that was just over six feet tall (a height I can quickly surmise since I am six feet tall). This designated area was meant for my soldiers, as it was an "orderly mess" of numerous bins, all of which were overflowing with freebies from countless care packages. At any hour of the day, soldiers could stop by and grab extra soap, snacks, toothbrushes—you name it. While deployed, my unit received an abundance of care packages that were crammed with just about anything and everything—and the CP was beginning to be littered with boxes, especially since we were approaching the month of December.

It was Sergeant Marco Vasquez who popped his head over his computer, my quiet, stellar NBC (nuclear, biological, chemical) sergeant who was also my driver on several convoys. He probably was swearing underneath his breath that he was the unlucky one, the only person in the office to answer my cranky question. My headquarters team caught on quickly that I was the most unpleasant after my morning beatings from Battalion, where I had to give my company's daily battlefield update briefs, and on top of that, I was currently embroiled in an unnecessary battle over my company's combat patch ceremony.

"Yes, ma'am. I think First Sergeant said it was a care package that was simply addressed to HHC."

Top walked into the CP at that moment, a to-go breakfast plate in hand, not missing a beat. "Good morning, ma'am. Yes, we still need to open it and see if we can identify the individual it belongs to, or if it is just a care package meant for the company."

I instantly had a flashback of those damn duffels and tough boxes that were left at the reserve center back in Texas—for years! To put it lightly, I was annoyed that it had already sat there for several days. So I grabbed the box, which was leaning against the wall, and I laid it on the ground. With one quick slice along the taped seam from my Benchmade knife, the smell of a fresh evergreen tree burst from the box and engulfed the room.

"What in the hell?" I wondered out loud.

With Top and Sergeant Vasquez peering over my shoulder, I unwrapped a live, six-foot-tall Douglas fir Christmas tree. The more and more I breathed in that glorious smell—an absolutely foreign fragrance on Bagram Airfield—I was overcome with joy and peace. I turned around to see that this tree was also having the same effect on Top and Vasquez—both had sloppy grins ear-to-ear.

Once we stood it up, and began to loosen the boughs, a card dropped to the floor.

I picked it up, and read, "To the Soldiers of HHC, enjoy this reminder of home during the Christmas season. Take care, (signed) Charles Eastman."

My husband had sent the live Christmas tree, the piece of home, and gifted it to my soldiers. He was wise enough to include a tree stand, tree skirt, and numerous strings of Christmas lights. Charles knew all too well what it felt like to be deployed over the holidays, considering he had spend the past two Christmases in Iraq. This was our third consecutive Christmas in which one of us was serving in combat; outside of our family and close friends, not many people knew this. Thus his gesture meant so much more to me. I was moved beyond words.

Charles is the epitome of the expression *quiet professional*. An unapologetic introvert with a ready switch to alpha-male when necessary, he is like many other soldiers serving in the military who grew up playing GI Joe. From his earliest years, he could be found camping in the rural woods of Maine and generally flourishing at any outdoor activity. He is smart as a whip, only matched by relentless perseverance to succeed at whatever he puts his mind to. He joined the military before 9/11 and continued to reenlist time and time again, because of his unshakable sense of duty.

Nonetheless, his self-proclaimed "peace-loving-hippy" family never encouraged him to become a soldier. In fact, his mother kept her dual citizenship to Canada for the specific reason that if there were ever another draft in the States, her son would have the option to avoid it. Vietnam had truly scared a generation. But what his parents did not realize at the time was their own beautiful examples of service had influenced their son to prioritize service too. In his own way—*sua sponte*. And that undercurrent of compassion from those dear "hippies" was part of his equation.

That compassion couldn't have come at a better time.

A deployment feels like three phases (or levels of hell), which I'll refer to as the first month, the grind, and the last month. Regardless of however long you are there, these three poignant stages still generally confine one's tour of duty. The first month is the shock phase, learning the ropes, settling in. The grind is the time in the middle, filled with the mundane to the unbelievable; days are blurred, and missing home and loved ones has turned into a constant, daily toothache. The last month is the most unpredictable; soldiers are so close to having the deployment behind them, and that sense of accomplishment may engender overconfidence or irreverent behavior. The first and the last months are the most dangerous, historically speaking, because that is when soldiers do not *know enough* or have been deployed *long enough*.

My company had just completed the first phase and was trudging into the grind—and the holiday season. Additionally, having recently passed the hallmark milestone of "thirty days in combat," several of my soldiers who were on their first deployment could now proudly don the coveted combat patch on the right shoulder of their uniform. A combat patch is a symbol to the world (well, mostly to other soldiers) that denotes wartime service, recognizing a soldier's participation in combat operations. Units often mark this rite of passage with a combat patch ceremony, yet plans for my company's formation had been stymied by an irascible command sergeant major who missed the whole point of the ritual by contaminating the moment with drama about what patch was *really* authorized. Although reserve and national guard units had been deploying to fight these wars from their beginning, it was still apparently confusing to some how to interpret the policy.

All of this prolonged the date for the ceremony and spiked frustrations within the battalion, as my soldiers anxiously awaited to learn what patch was sanctioned. I knew my soldiers needed the formation—they deserved to be honored. Further, recognizing their feat would engender pride, which would arouse a much-needed dose of motivation as we moved into the grind (and the holiday season). Every day that passed that thirty-day mark— with no guidance from our higher command on what patch to wear—sapped morale from my soldiers (especially those on their first deployment). The impasse was finally resolved by legal counsel musings on the combat patch policy, of course with vague and circuitous reasoning. After thirty-seven days in combat, at five o'clock (1700 in army-speak) on a Wednesday afternoon, I was finally permitted to acknowledge my soldiers' accomplishment. Following the ceremony, my soldiers helped decorate their live Christmas tree (and were invigorated by the smell of it!)—all of which was perfect timing.

I observed several techniques that soldiers applied to help them persevere during the immeasurable hardships of a combat deployment: we kept putting one foot in front of the other, for each other and those we had lost; some attended church, believed in prayer; some performed regular exercise (and released those endorphins); while others clung to what they had back home or what they would do once they returned home. I was no stranger to all of these options on how to survive the deployment, in addition to fighting cantankerous individuals on behalf of my soldiers, so they could enjoy the simple distraction of a combat patch ceremony. My faith and motivation were wide-ranging and ever evolving, and, of course, challenged like everyone else. And as others have experienced, what lifted my spirit on any given day was often unexpected.

On the thirty-seventh day in combat, I found that what motivated me was a string of Christmas lights. After a long day that ended with yet another rocket attack, since we received rocket attacks on base that night, I sat on my bed quietly, thinking. I began to take off my boots, and empty the numerous compartments on my uniform when I realized that I had an extra string of white lights in my cargo pocket. I had shoved them in there earlier that evening when the company was decorating the Christmas tree. I pulled them out, and immediately plugged them in. The glow warmed my soul, and for the remainder of my time in Afghanistan, those lights were taped on the plywood wall by my bed.

On some of the more difficult days, when I finally made it to my CHU, exhausted and deflated, those lights would help me recall the joy and peace that overcame me when I first smelled that Douglas fir. They inspired me and were a reminder of so many things that encouraged me, from thinking about my remarkable soldiers and the night they proudly decorated the Christmas tree (right shoulder fully outfitted with combat patches), to my faith in God, His treasured presence, and what the promise of a new life brought to the world (due to their holiday connection to Christmas). Finally, the Christmas lights made me feel closer to home, closer to Charles, and his sincere act of love.

JOURNAL ENTRY FOR 01 DECEMBER 2009

> *"O Christmas tree, O Christmas tree . . ."*
>
> You'd be surprised how much you will start thinking about trees when it feels like you're enclosed in a desert parking lot. Hands down, my favorite tree in the entire world is a Christmas tree—even beating out an aspen, Joshua, magnolia, palm, or eucalyptus! It's the connection to the holiday, and how Christmas has become even more special since Charles proposed on Christmas Eve in 2003. However, this will be the third Christmas in a row that we are separated by deployments. How do you find any good or positive when you consider that? Well, Charles gave me a way . . . he sent a live Christmas tree from the US!
>
> It stands six feet tall, and is absolutely beautiful. I am so touched, especially since his heartfelt gift was intended for all my soldiers to enjoy. I know the holidays are harder for loved ones back home, and hope Charles can get some time off work to be with his parents this year. I couldn't even

email or call to thank him for the tree because the Internet and phones were down tonight. Ahhh! I also wanted to tell him I can finally honor my soldiers and hold a formation for the combat patch ceremony tomorrow. It is nice to not have to deal with this issue (or the person who instigated the ridiculous spectacle), and to put more energy on everything else. I guess it works out because now my soldiers can enjoy the Christmas tree after the ceremony tomorrow night.

We had to put the tree in the chaplain's office because it was too large to fit in the CP. I'll make sure to swing by each day to get a whiff of that live fir. Thank you, Charles. I love you and miss you, like Christmas.

JOURNAL ENTRY FOR 02 DECEMBER 2009

"Rocket attacks and our combat patch ceremony"

IDF (indirect fire) again tonight, around ten o'clock, just hours after our combat patch ceremony. I clearly heard the launch of six rockets from behind the hospital that is under construction, the one that is right behind our living and work area known as Dragon Village. Some of my soldiers said they saw the rockets overhead when they ran outside. As far as we know now, no one was hurt. I have full accountability of my company, thank God.

The formation earlier tonight was just what I had hoped it would be—those not on shift who attended had a great time, relishing a tradition that supposedly has been around since the Civil War. We had the 82nd Airborne patches piled into a Kevlar, and as each squad posted, I put the patch on the right shoulder of every soldier, shaking their hand and saluting them for being here. Afterwards, it was fun seeing how the teams creatively assembled ornaments for the Christmas tree. Charles, I am so thankful for you, and for your thoughtfulness. I wonder how you are handling my being over here . . . I know it is excruciating for the person back home. I know that all too well. My heart has a scaly layer over it, over here. There's not much time to stop and think about it all, especially when we stay distracted by regular rocket attacks, missions . . . Today was a reminder how the people around you can become family when you are away from home, especially during hardship.

Tonight, I am going to fall asleep looking at this extra string of white Christmas lights plugged in by my bed, and just take a deep breath . . .

JOURNAL ENTRY FOR 02 APRIL 2010

"Tree"

Today I found overwhelming confidence and trust in the most unlikely people and activity. It began this morning, sitting down with the BC. As much as it feels like I'm the first in line for the beatings with her (I am, after all, the HHC commander), she was remarkably supportive of my stance on Sergeant Jose Jimenez's evaluation. It's criminal how much time I've had to waste fighting over the wording on his potential. I have assessed that he should be "promoted as soon as possible," whereas the irascible person who also has a say holds a grudge with him because he opted to not reenlist (and she wants that removed from his evaluation, as she sniped, "he's not staying in, so remove his potential for promotion"). But this evaluation is for the present, and should not be influenced by this soldier's future path. It looks like the end is in sight, and the BC will back me (and Jimenez).

I snuck away for a nap during the lunch hour today, and that helped fight the constant fatigue . . . well, a little. What was extremely refreshing was going to a yoga class at the air force gym this evening. Tara asked me to go with her, and it was her kind insistence in her request that made me make time. Tara is a true role model, even for me (as her boss), in how she strives to insert activities that balance the insanity—she unfailingly attends church, and now she is incorporating this yoga class. After I mastered the tree stance tonight, I understand why she attends these classes. Yoga is relaxing and uplifting. Just what I needed, since later tonight we received another rocket attack on base.

This time, I was on the phone with Charles, and he heard the blasts. It was pretty loud. I know he was alarmed, and it's upsetting for him to know what I'm going through. Needless to say, we ended our call, and I got back to my CP to make sure we had full accountability. All was well. The sound of helicopters circling overhead makes me miss Charles even more . . . good luck finding those POO's [point of origin]. I have four to five months left, over here ... and I pray for angels.

In a few days, I will convoy the MATV (MRAP lite) to Morales-Frazier, then Kutchbach. I am no exception to the superstitious tendencies over here, and have tucked the guidon in my pack to go on every battlefield rotation. It now has quite a few miles and convoys between those seams. It somehow reassures me when I'm seriously exposed to danger, to know that my company is with me (the guidon being that symbol), and that I am doing this for them. When I return home, and perform my change of command, it will mean all the more to see that guidon passed forward, knowing all these stories are with it. Hopefully, then, Charles and I can find some time to relax, "on the coast of somewhere beautiful, trade winds blowing through my hair . . ."

JOURNAL ENTRY FOR 04 APRIL 2010

"It doesn't feel like Sunday, it feels like hell"

There are some soldiers you can never forget, and the warrant officer in my company who said this today is one of them. Chief Warrant Officer Kristy James dazzles people with her brilliance, and shocks them with her honesty. I love it. I passed her on the way to Easter service this morning, and wished her a happy Sunday. She laughed her unforgettable laugh, and that was her response. It was so matter-of-fact, oh well, here we go . . .

Another one of my soldiers reached out to me and asked me to join her for mass. It was Sergeant Becerra this time, Brandi's pal and one of my first "profiles in courage." It was nice to sit in church with someone I knew (and liked), although that comfort lapsed when I turned around toward the end of mass to wish "peace be with you" to the imposing colonel in the pew behind me (my senior rater, no less). It was a good message, from the same priest who encouraged us to not *take away* during this Lent season, but to *add to* instead. He wisely pointed out that we are already giving up so much to be over here. So I've added to my life, from yoga with Tara to occasional lunchtime naps to help boost my energy for the remainder of the day. Four hours of sleep at night just doesn't cut it.

And, of course, I'm adding more prayer. Although we had yet another night of rocket attacks, I thank you, God, for keeping my soldiers safe. Today doesn't feel like Easter; then again, holidays in general have lost their "feel." I know that's due to the fact that I've lost so many holidays. Too many have been spent alone, away from loved ones, in desolate places like this hellhole. At least tonight, as I lie in bed exhausted, I still have these Christmas lights . . . and I will fall asleep with a smile, recalling that hilarious quip earlier today from Kristy.

When you know that you're loved,
it frees you up. It is a source of power.

You may only see one set of footprints,
nevertheless trust that God always shows up.

You have absolute power over your
motivation—it is in your hands.

As a precaution though, keep an extra
string of Christmas lights handy!

★ ★ ★

Asking the Right Questions

"Are the French playing nice?" I asked.

I knew the answer from Rick's laugh. Staff Sergeant Rick Groff was one of my best soldiers and a team leader for one of my intelligence collection teams located at Morales-Frazier, a forward operations base in eastern Afghanistan run by the French.

It was a few weeks into our deployment, and Rick was providing an update on his team and their mission. His insight was always impeccable, tempered by a prior deployment to Iraq as an infantry soldier and a civilian career back home as a police officer, keeping Texas safe. Furthermore, I had another layer of confidence in Rick since I knew him well. Years earlier, on his first weekend as a reserve soldier, I served with him in Charlie Company. He was a stand-up, collaborative, hard-working, optimistic soldier who loved to share funny stories about his kids. He always felt like my kid brother, too, and I knew I was extremely lucky to have him leading one of my teams in a kinetic and critical area of operations.

As we were wrapping up our call, Rick added, "Ma'am, I also gave your contact information to the ODA commander, Jason.[54] He wants to talk about synchronizing our collection effort and utilizing a few of my team's interrogators, especially Taylor."

Perfect, I thought. ODA was jargon for a Special Forces team, and having spent time working in the special operations community, it came as no surprise to me that these guys were reaching out to a new intelligence asset in theater, one that had female soldiers. After talking with Jason, my presumption was confirmed, as one of the first things he said to me was, "I am so excited your unit has female interrogators! Finally, we can now add roughly 50 percent of the population to the table."

You see, Jason knew from one too many deployments that the prohibitive culture in the Middle East did not allow males who were not family members to talk with females. Thus, when female soldiers participated in missions, whether they were village patrols or attending *jirgas* [tribal meetings], they could at the very least talk and interact with the female population. Perhaps it was his devotion to his own two daughters back home, but Jason understood females were just as important as males, and he saw firsthand how that translated on the battlefield. Further, he recognized that what made females *different* from men was an advantage on the battlefield. Just as the Navajo Code Talkers, a group of Native Americans who served in the marines during World War II, offered a unique skill set that aided combat operations, so, too, do women—they were and are on the front lines and changing the tide of war simply by their differentiation quality.

I served with soldiers who were overqualified and more than prepared to face the challenges of combat—and they were both male and female. I also served with soldiers who got in their own way, did not fulfill their potential, and should not have been in a combat zone, let alone the military—and they were both male and female. As a commander, when deciding what positions my soldiers would fulfill, I asked myself if they had the required skills needed to perform their job so that it would result in mission success.[55] It is my belief that if any soldier can meet the (same) standards of a position, then he or she should have the opportunity to fulfill the responsibilities of that position.

Our military is fortunate that it has had women step up, volunteer, and honorably fulfill the mission-critical roles that were not *manned* post 9/11 due to staggering personnel shortages. More than one unit scheduled to deploy in support of the global war on terrorism would have been deemed operationally incapable if it weren't for the females who filled the ranks and positions on their battle rosters. Yet no one anticipated how females (roughly 15 percent of the force) who were fulfilling support roles would be subject to the same hardships and challenges of direct action positions after 9/11.[56]

Thousands of military woman were on those blurred front lines, numbers unlike any generation has seen before, and many displayed their fortitude and were awarded Combat Action Badges, Purple Hearts, Air Medals, Bronze Stars, the Distinguished Flying Cross, and Silver Stars.[57] Females in my company drove MRAPs on routes notorious for frequent IEDs and ambushes, they unearthed weapon caches near fields peppered with land mines, and patrolled villages to establish contact with that "other half of the population" we so desperately needed to know. We were alongside our male counterparts, brave, every step of the way.

After 9/11, females made the sacrifice like every other male in uniform, and some made the ultimate sacrifice, as generations of service members have done in every other war. I served with women of all ages, from all walks of life, who answered the call to serve in uniform and in combat. Some were fresh out of high school or college; others were mothers of infants, toddlers, tweens, or teens. They were single women to single moms, and sometimes they were wives who served alongside their husbands.[58] They were all someone's daughter or friend. They are all someone we should be proud of—and fully acknowledge—like every other service member who raised his right hand.

One of the most important lessons I learned working with interrogators is that you need to make sure you are asking the right questions. I often hear people ask if females are physically capable, if they have sexual discretion, or emotional control. Most of the conversations that center around such concerns typically close with the final question, as if to soften the preconceived idea that females are somehow inadequate, "Aren't we setting women up for failure if we open all positions to them?" What we should be asking is if we are setting our mission up for failure if it is performed without women.

Those in Special Operations began to ask that very question a few years into these wars, and were the pioneers on how the military can thoughtfully integrate a female effort into our force. Cultural support teams comprised of female soldiers served to enable military operations.[59] Yet should we stop there? Wherever our military may roam in the future, nearly half of the population in this world remains female. Should we *really* stop at strides like only opening the doors for women in occupational specialties like aviation, where the illusion that women are still somewhat removed from direct ground combat appeases some? It's just an illusion. Rocket-propelled grenades, heat-seeking missiles, and bullets know no gender.

As far as those who question the feasibility of female integration because women are more of a distraction than an asset, I would ask to consider how distractions of any nature are fundamentally a failure in leadership and, or, code of conduct. Unit cohesion can very well be achieved with diversity, and one's ability to stay focused on the mission is not contingent upon anatomy.[60] Women, in some way, have been an asset—in every single war. Women are not ill prepared, or insufficiently designed to succeed in the military—or in combat. They are not *really* the underdogs. The underdog, after all, can win and will win.[61]

All people can add value.

We must evolve as a force, and continually strive to not only accomplish our mission today, but also to accomplish the mission we will have in the future.[62] The truth is, that mission will have to be undertaken, again, by volunteers. The Frontline Generation is unique in that it was an all-volunteer military, and we should honor the spirit of that service by allowing people who are willing to go back and forth on multiple deployments the simple choice of choosing their military occupational specialty. We should permit all service members the opportunity to at least compete for assignments and not be excluded based on their gender. Service members should be excluded if they do not meet the *same* standards for that position.

We would be remiss if we do not acknowledge what has already happened—the Frontline Generation served all together in combat—and policy must catch up with reality.[63]

After all, an exclusion policy does not align with American values.[64] Diversity is a pillar of our society; it makes our country exceptional and has helped make our military the best in the world. We need to ask ourselves if the negative affects or lost opportunities that will ensue if we continue to separate women from all military ranks is a wise course of action. In his history of the interesting life of Charles George Gordon, Irish-born Sir William Francis Butler, a general in the nineteenth-century British army, wrote, "The nation that will insist on drawing a broad line of demarcation between the fighting man and the thinking man is liable to find its fighting done by fools and its thinking done by cowards." In that same spirit, a military that separates its ranks by gender will remain an incomplete force.

JOURNAL ENTRY FOR 17 MARCH 2010

"Weapons cache recovery with SPC Ashley Johnson"

I guess today is St. Patrick's Day. Nevertheless, I had my mind on other things. I went on a mission with HCT 21 this afternoon. Specialist Ashley Johnson was in charge, an extremely bright and energetic young woman in her early twenties. She has a naturally happy, calm disposition, is athletic, and is a strikingly beautiful black woman. The Taliban fighters she interrogates succumb every time, as the shock of her very *female* presence surprises them and gives her the upper hand and power. On top of that, she is one of the best in the (interrogation) booth.

Ahh, the mission today . . . where do I begin? Due to Ashley's professional savvy to perform her job well, the team is now credited with recovering a weapons cache of over 600 fuses, munitions, and weapon systems. It was in a local village outside BAF. And it was outright impressive to watch Ashley in action. First, the local national that is riding along in the back of an MRAP with the maneuver element would tell the translator something. The translator would pass that information to Ashley, and she would pass that along to the truck commander, who then directed his driver . . . and yes, as you can guess, the driver most likely already passed the turn once the information went through four people.

After several "detours," which are not the most comforting experience in a convoy in a combat zone, we made it to the location, in which the convoy came to a security halt and the local national pointed us to the location along a hillside where the cache was stored. Of course, this cache was in a "cleared" landmine field from the Soviet War. At the end of the day, a controlled detonation by EOD destroyed the cache.

Unfortunately we didn't recover enough today because at 2300 tonight we received IDF, again. I was in the shower this time; another rocket attack and thankfully, 100 percent accountability of all personnel. I can't wait to tell my family and friends about this day. They would be proud, and I couldn't be more proud of Ashley. Because of her efforts, her ability to perform her job well, there are fewer weapons on the battlefield, especially those that can get into the wrong hands and be used against innocent civilians or us. Today was worth it!

JOURNAL ENTRY FOR 20 MAY 2010

"It's a big deal"

Nothing like starting your day sitting in a mission brief that you are about to go on, but it is entirely in a language you do not speak. Thanks to an elaborate sand table, body language, and Taylor (one of the soldiers on my intelligence collection team who is fluent in French), you got the gist that "we" the good guys were going to talk with "them" the bad guys (Taliban sympathizers, probably fighters).

I am on FOB Kutchbach, another base solely run and operated by the French. My five-person team (and the only Americans on the mission) convoyed our MATV alongside a French infantry unit and Afghan National Army unit, and participated in a dismounted patrol deeper into Bendreni Valley today. Once in the village, ANA received small arms fire. We were tucked into the village and stood by until close air support arrived. Wow. That got your attention, and the shooting stopped for the most part, which allowed us to continue our meeting with local village elders. Since my team was utilizing the interpreter, the only way I could communicate with the children sitting near the meeting (there was not a woman in sight) was by sharing a pack of gum. I made origami birds out of the wrappers, and they ran off with them, smiling. We always leave an impression, so hopefully that one sticks.

It is a beautiful landscape here, yet you feel like you are going back in time. *Centuries* back in time. When we returned, the team had dinner together and another toast to not crashing the MATV, since we drove blacked out again (no headlights, in the dark), and held our breath on those "oh shit" moments in which that top-heavy monstrosity of a vehicle lumbered its way back to the FOB on narrow dirt roads. After dinner, it was great seeing that the ODA guys had safely returned to the FOB too. Unfortunately, I faced a rather awkward moment because I saw entirely too much of one of them.

Converted trailers that have shower stalls and toilets are scattered throughout the base, but since there are so few females on these forward bases, bathrooms are shared. Sometimes there is a sign on the front door (male/female) that you can flip over, other times you open the door and announce you are entering so that anyone else in the stalls is apprised. Well, I announced that I was going into the bathroom but one of the sergeants stepped out of the shower at the exact moment I walked it. As we both awkwardly scrambled to turn away and apologize, I nearly broke my neck getting out of that trailer in a hurry.

Oh, I felt so bad—and I saw everything! I knew the ODA team fairly well since they were the only other Americans on the FOB, besides a worthless LNO [liaison officer] from division. From sharing reports with their intel guy who had recently shown me a photograph of his new baby boy, to sharing meals with their armorer who passed me a new rear site for my rifle—these guys were like brothers. From the grumpy master sergeant who looked just like the lead singer in Metallica, to doing planks in the gym with their comms guy who was a PT stud, I knew them well. I had hitchhiked rides on their convoys back to BAF, and went through rocket attacks with them on Valentine's Day. Moreover, they felt like an extension of my family, since they were part of the community of quiet professionals who served with my husband.

The (naked) sergeant beat me to his team leader (after he got dressed, I presume). Craig, his commander and my counterpart, told me that, apparently, the sergeant was more embarrassed and concerned that he might have offended me. When I spoke with Craig later this evening, he was cool as a cat, kept laughing, and said, "Don't worry about it." I remember saying, "Craig, be serious for a minute! Should I go apologize to him?' He said, "No, just forget about it." That's when my selection of word choice could have been better. I said, "Come on, Craig, it's a big deal. I should apologize, right?" Craig burst out laughing. He quickly replied, "Oh, it's a 'big deal,' huh?" Geesh. I am not only going to have to apologize for catching this sergeant off guard in the bathroom, but also have to apologize for the new nickname (Big Deal) that he is surely going to get from this day forward. At least we can all end this day with a laugh.

Try to think about things from every angle, and turn questions around and upside-down to ensure you are getting at the right answer.

"Why not" is just as important to ask as "Why."

Gender does not define you. It differentiates you— and differentiation adds value.

Always knock twice before entering a shared bathroom. That helps make it "not a big deal."

★ ★ ★

Close Calls Don't Discriminate

This is a story you've seen before. Now, you can read what happens next . . .

On a cold morning in December of 2009, I met up with two of my sergeants from one of my thirteen teams at a main gate along the perimeter of Bagram Airfield, Afghanistan. My soldiers and I were filling a few empty seats on what was considered a routine patrol by an agriculture development team. The convoy and the mission had us stopping in Mahmud-i-Raqi, the village that is the crossroads to Main Supply Route (MSR) Nevada and MSR Vermont.

My joining the convoy on that morning served two purposes. One, I could observe my soldiers on a mission in which they were collecting information from everything on the local geography to people, in order to help solve the puzzle of *priority intelligence requirements*. Second, it would also give me a chance to do a route reconnaissance, since that was the same road I would take in a few days with a different intelligence team of mine scheduled to convoy to a French operations base in Kapisa Province.

On that particular day, the routes were considered a medium threat level, with some activity of small-arms fire but not really a threat for improvised explosive devices, known as IEDs, or roadside bombs. Nonetheless, a few additional MRAPs were lined up at the front of the convoy, and their equipment and the unit patches on their uniforms immediately identified them as EOD—Explosives Ordinance Disposal. Bomb detectors. Apparently, a local national had called in throughout the night, warning US forces an IED might be emplaced in a culvert along the route. Now, these types of tips are not uncommon, and not always accurate—yet all of them are taken seriously. The individual had even provided an approximate grid coordinate.

With more than fifty pounds of additional weight from my body armor, extra ammunition, and two locked and loaded weapons (an M9 Beretta and M4 rifle), I climbed into the second MRAP with Sergeant Jesse Miller, claiming the two empty seats in the back. I had known this blond, blue-eyed Texan for a few years, ever since he reported to my company fresh out of basic training. I had shaken his parents' hands a few months earlier at our farewell ceremony back home and told them I would take care of their son.

That responsibility felt heavier than it had ever been, since a few weeks earlier, on a similar brisk, early morning, we had paid our last respects to a fallen comrade at an unforgettable ramp ceremony—one who had lost his life when his MRAP drove over an IED. Jesse had helped carry the flag-draped coffin.

These were all things you try to *not* think about before a mission, and our mission was still a go. Jesse looked over at me and smiled as we left the relative safety of the base. I wondered if perhaps my impeccably bright soldier was more comfortable going "outside the wire" because he spoke Pashto. Being fluent in the native language would be pretty damn helpful right now, I thought. I stayed focused by listening to the occasional squawk or static from our headsets, as the truck commander provided constant updates on our progress.

It feels like forever when you're driving to a destination marked with an IED.

As our convoy neared the site, the lead truck in front of us came to an abrupt security halt, and over the radios I heard, "Oh shit, I think we passed the grid. The location is actually about a hundred meters behind us. All trucks, check if you have a culvert by you and do not stop near one."

Jesse and I looked out the bulletproof glass window in the back door of our MRAP, and lo and behold, a few feet behind our truck was a culvert.

With direct and explicit language, we relayed the message to our driver to pull forward. We climbed out of the MRAP, and spent the next few hours at a security halt outside the local village. All the while, EOD inspected the site with their robots and blast suits.

I can still remember how the body armor pinched at my waist, or collarbone, as I continuously alternated how I tightened the flat plates that teeter-tottered one way or another on my chest. And how the only laugh that I had that day was when I asked one of the Kentucky guardsmen who was part of our convoy to pull security for me so that I could go relieve myself off the path. He said, "Ma'am, I've never seen a female pee before." I responded, "Don't worry, you'll only hear it because you're going to look the opposite direction and pull security. And, spoiler alert, pee sounds like pee."

There wasn't much to laugh about once we learned that the culvert we had just driven over, and parked in front of, did indeed have a command wire IED hidden underneath the road. EOD (and OSI—Air Force Office of Special Investigations) found and removed the cylinder with all its wires and fuses. They suspect we must have been early that morning, because the final step in connecting the bomb to the command wire was not complete. Call it luck, or chance, or whatever you will—we couldn't think about it too much on that day because we still had a mission to complete.

That was approximately eight hours, of only one day, of ten months that I was deployed as a commander in combat in Afghanistan. And no two days were the same. I can't emphasize enough that I did not see the worst of it, because every veteran has been moved by a harrowing combat story, and every soldier in my company had our fallen brother on our minds. Yet while we served alongside each other, what unknowingly happened is that in some sense, courage, or mettle was being acquired. Because we all faced a degree of close calls by the very essence of being deployed to a combat zone—it's the nature of the job.

In fact, this culvert moment itself is not necessarily that unique to a veteran, since most of us have ended up in tight spots that are uncomfortable, to put it mildly. For example, several months later, I watched my battalion commander pin a combat action badge on the breasts of four of my soldier's uniforms (Sergeants Eldridge and Lopez being two of them) because they rightly qualified when a rocket landed near their CHU—while they were sleeping—and fortunately detonated six feet underground because it was so moist from three days of rain. Like that night, or the mission with Jesse, we were all as different as one could imagine: young and not so young; enlisted and officers; male and female; Latino and Caucasians; first deployment to multiple tours; fathers, daughters, or newly engaged.

We were soldiers who were all indiscriminately exposed. Because serving in uniform after 9/11 meant there were no front lines—we were all out front. And all those close calls did not discriminate. More importantly, those close calls helped make us stronger.

As author Malcolm Gladwell asserted in his book, *David & Goliath*, the catastrophic error of the London bombings in World War II is that the Germans thought the trauma associated with the Blitz would destroy the courage of the British people.

In fact, it did the opposite. It created a city of remote misses,
who were more courageous than they had ever been before...
Courage is not something that you already have that
makes you brave when the tough times start. Courage is
what you earn when you've been through the tough times
and you discover they aren't so tough after all.[65]

That discovery is not necessarily immediate. Because the morning I rolled into Bagram from a six-hour extended convoy sitting next to Sergeant Joel Lundy, I was not ready to qualify that night as *not* that tough.

Joel was one of the two infantry soldiers on my battle roster who was not only a proud father of several girls (I couldn't keep count), but a grandfather. He begged our BC to include him on the battle roster, and she was able to waive his occupational specialty (he was an infantry guy in an intelligence slot) because he led my unattended ground sensor team. Lundy maximized the intelligence equipment and mission because he brought the infantry perspective. He was calm, easygoing, and all about common sense. And we spent a night in purgatory when our midnight convoy broke down twice.

We were just trying to hitchhike our way back to BAF after delivering an MRAP to the FOB Morales-Frazier team earlier that week. We jumped on a convoy with the Georgia National Guard who was heading back to BAF with all their equipment shoved into four MRAPs and three local jingle trucks. We knew the routes were showing heightened activity that night, and the French route clearance unit had gone through MSR Vermont to Mahmud-i-Raqi, the more dangerous stretch, and unearthed an unexploded ordinance earlier that morning.

Not even an hour into the drive, one of the jingle trucks in our convoy broke down—naturally along a narrow mountain road with steep cliffs screaming above us and then dropping dramatically on the other side of our MRAP. We were stuck between switchbacks with very little radio communications, on the outskirts of one of the most dangerous villages along the route; troops had been ambushed there a few days earlier. Told to stay in our vehicles, Lundy and I listened to the buzzing of close air support helicopters overhead as we waited three hours for a recovery team. You can imagine a lot can be said, and not said, in hours like that. What we unanimously decided halfway into it was to eat most of the French croissants we'd grabbed from the French chow hall, which I had planned to deliver to the colonel. Talk about comfort food.

After giving up on waiting for a recovery team, the Georgia Guardsmen scrounged up a simple chain, and one of their MRAP Cougars towed that worthless forty-foot jingle truck. But not much further down the road, the MRAP that Lundy and I were in broke down—a gas leak! Thankfully we were the last vehicle, and the crew was able to attach a tow bar to the MRAP in front of us while Lundy and I pulled rear security.

Spending more than an hour staring into the eerie dark night with the certainty that others were staring back at us, I knew the only reason we were not engaged was because of the steady circling of Apaches and Kiowas overhead. I also knew that if anything were to happen that night, I wanted Lundy to get home to all those daughters of his. It was one of those moments you know it's *absolutely* about the person next to you. Lundy was my sense of purpose—not politics or policies that had me in the middle of Afghanistan that cold, unforgettable night.

We were so very different.

Or were we? Because nights like that, just like the early morning convoy with Jesse when we drove over the IED, taught me it was all about what we have in common. In those moments—survival.

And, so much more, such as common ethos, common training, and a common commitment.

Further, we were all absolutely ordinary—from Jesse, to me, to Lundy—from your home state or your schools. But through service we transcended that category to transform into extraordinary people who persevered through the tough times. I learned on those convoys what psychologist Angela Duckworth described in her research on grit, that what distinguishes high performers is that you don't turn to something easier when faced with struggle.[66] Instead, embrace the challenge, or as we say in the military, embrace the suck. We are now stronger than others, stronger than we were before.

JOURNAL ENTRY FOR 16 DECEMBER 2009

"Convoy to Morales-Frazier"

We safely convoyed to FOB M-F today with the 410 MP Unit. Their four MRAPSs and our one trekked across rolling hills and up jagged mountains (called switchbacks), with sections of the road washed out from the last week's storms. Not to mention the wild goats, countless Afghan onlookers, and wild-eyed children waving or not waving. Sergeant Vasquez was the driver, my quiet guy who did really well. Sergeant Kimball—the radio guru—was a comforting addition due to his ease on the comms. Sergeant Lundy was the gunner, and his 11Bravo (infantry) skills were a needed addition. Staff Sergeant Schmitty, my OMT leader who was a rock, was a passenger. I was the truck commander (TC).

Just before our SP, Sergeant Eldridge ran down to our staging site with a spot report that local Taliban were staging an ambush of our route with fifty fighters. Those threats are hit or miss—the route has had IEDs and, more commonly, small arms fire recently. But today, the angels were present. God, I am so thankful nothing happened. Before we drove off, Sergeant Mac sought me out to wish me well, and said, "Ok Brave heart, you come back to us with that smile— be safe." I thought that was so touching, so sincere. His sentiment left me speechless.

It felt good to be a TC, to do well, and do good by my guys— my incredible crew. I was proud of them. It was great arriving to M-F and I've already said *bonjour* to several. Staff Sergeant Greenfield said I could crash in his room because he's currently at BAF (there are no extra bunks so, it was nice everyone could squeeze in with the team on this base). Oh .. . here's to eight hours of sleep tonight! First, a grateful prayer while I hold this angel pendant that hangs around my neck, which I have worn every day of this deployment . . . with a prayer inscribed on the back: "Watch over and guide me."

JOURNAL ENTRY FOR 17 DECEMBER 2009

"Have a little faith in me . . ."

Busy day on the FOB. One of the members on my HCT out here is Corporal Lauren Taylor. She is such a gem—so smart, unassuming, and a really fantastic soldier. She's from Penn-sylvania, joined the reserves initially as a medical supply specialist right out of high school, finished her college degree in DC, and is perfectly fluent in French. Exactly what we need on a French FOB, as she is essential in translating mission critical reports every day! The army is so fortunate to have such a stellar volunteer. I continue to marvel at what amazing citizens serve our country so selflessly. I am honored to be in their company, not just for them to be in mine. She's one story of many I can share about the soldiers on this team, yet I'll spend time bragging about her tonight. By the way, chow halls on French FOBs have Brie cheese and crème de la crème dessert dishes. Not to mention alcohol. And, of course, French soldiers gave Taylor two birds in a cage that they bought off the local bazaar. I trust her and the rest of my team out here (and I told them that) to make the right decision on all those suitors to the seduction of a few drinks. I trust that Rick, my team leader, will hold them together.

JOURNAL ENTRY FOR 21 DECEMBER 2009

"Jingle (truck) all the way . . ."

A two-day trip to a FOB can easily turn to five when weather rolls in or rotary is rerouted to support operations. Yet today we received the go-ahead that we could convoy with the PMT (police mentor team), a National Guard unit from Georgia (at the last hour, and on their final trip back to BAF before they redeploy). I was surprised the BC approved it–she really is trying to not be risk averse and she is supporting me to be a leader "from the front"—so I thank God for that (keep your hand on the BC's heart).

Our SP was 1900 with ETA of 2030, which was much better than the Blue Ring Route later tonight, which was a pickup at 2230, and then after you fly the whole damn route, you would stumble off the '47 at BAF around 0230. Granted, air is preferred to convoys, of course. Especially these days, the routes between BAF and M-F have not been looking good either—heightened activity with ambushes, small arms fire, and IEDs riddling the "potential" reports every day. The French route clearance did go through MSR Vermont to Mahmud-i-Raqi, the more dangerous stretch, and unearthed a UXO this morning. Talk about bad signs from the get-go.

Should have taken the cold helicopter ride because we didn't arrive to BAF until after 0200 due to *two* broken-down vehicles and no recovery team. After being sitting ducks for three hours, you would expect this night to end badly. At one point, the truck commander observed that he was getting messages (or so he thought) from some of the Apaches flying overhead because they were asking Longbow 06 her status on Blue Force Tracker. That's when it dawned on me, "Hey, that's my call sign, please type back what's going on." It was indeed a message from my JOC at BAF concerned about the delay. It was not the Apaches circling overhead.

We should have been engaged, on the edge of the most dangerous village, with four MRAPS and three jingle trucks in our convoy. But, from my assessment, the fact that we had CAS almost from the instant the first vehicle broke down till we rolled in to BAF was what made a difference. Apaches and Kiowas were swooping over and by our switchbacks, and followed us all the way home—for six hours. After tonight, if I ever have to be stuck in hell for six hours, I know Lundy would be on my list of people I know I could make it through with. He was solid as a rock. Thank you God for all the angels, especially CAS tonight.

JOURNAL ENTRY FOR 22 DECEMBER 2009

"How to top breaking down in a combat zone in the middle of the night"

Wow, what a warm welcome back, by all. Not to mention a few unexpected hugs and we-missed-yous. Someone mentioned the BC was even worried about me last night. I hope the trip last night did not alarm her because I need to keep leading from the front. Speaking of that, HCT 21 secured another weapons cache today and this one had a big fish—a surface to air missile (SA-7). It was so fulfilling to know and see my guys get such a score—meaning so much more to this aviator's wife. Sam worked with a local national and did an impeccable job! This is their ninth weapons recovery mission in two months—breaking every record. Sam, my team leader, is absolutely exceptional. A great guy, quiet and humble. Deeply smart, reminds me a lot of my older brother Travis—looks like him too. I am so proud to serve with him. He saved countless lives today. That's a day worth more than we'll ever know.

JOURNAL ENTRY FOR 18 JUNE 2010

"Man, I've got to get out of this town . . ."

I know the songwriter was definitely not in combat when he wrote this, but I guess that's a testament that hell is hell wherever you are. Or, as Tara asked me recently, "Can you explain purgatory?" My best attempt at doing so was saying, "Yeah, look around."

So many things to do before I head home on R&R in a few days; what I didn't expect today was the unexpected kudos from Texas who told me I was an excellent company commander and that I've come a long way. I've learned you must go the distance to grow. And growth is a choice. I chose yes. It's easy to do that when you have so many reasons to. I think my count at this point for my company is over 110. I have 110 reasons. I also know that any one of them may not be here when I return. From Schmitty sitting on that atrocious brown couch in my CP every night providing excellent updates on the forward deployed teams, to Tara and Starkey . . . all of them. Yet I know I need to go. The season of change lingers, the good-byes have started, as we are near the end of our tour, and I am taking one of the very last R&R spots. Your soldiers must eat and rest before you—always.

Oh, to those good-byes—I said mine to Craig tonight. He will leave Afghanistan while I am home, so we'll miss each other before I return from leave. I thanked him for all he taught me, for being the Special Forces example that I believed was real all along, and, especially, for keeping an eye out and *watching out* for my soldiers on his FOB. Having that trust was paramount. He said he'd contact me immediately if anything happens while I'm gone. I pray the angels hold tight while I am away. It was sad to say good-bye. Like other brief, fleeting, raw collisions over here, it feels cut short, as if there's more to unearth. Only God knows who shows up again, who will remain a fixture, and I believe He waits patiently, until we grasp that the good life lies within. In a few hours, I'll be on a plane, on my way out of this place . . . out of this pain.

★ ★ ★

Turn life into a remote miss.
Allow it to make you stronger.

You are never too old or too young to serve.

Never go on a convoy in a combat zone with a
person who can't properly find a grid coordinate.

This translates in life; especially when you are
on a road that is tough, make sure you have the
right people in your vehicle, on your team. And
that they are giving you the best directions.

★ ★ ★

Never Shower Alone

"Ma'am, I'm at a good stopping point on the property book review—may I head over to the chaplain's office with Captain Hernandez? We wanted to watch a movie tonight."

Tara, my company XO, was probably one of the hardest-working lieutenants on Bagram. Another vivacious Texan (and a redhead too), she was my right-hand (wo)man, primarily responsible for managing my company's very large property books and anything else I threw at her, since she was my backup. She rarely had downtime for these things called movies. She was, truly, the perfect lieutenant for that position, because she was a sleuth, a sponge, loyal, and she maintained military bearing (Captain Hernandez was her pal, Rod; however she continued to refer to a senior officer by title in the appropriate setting). I can't forget to mention she also had a great attitude in wearing the ball-and-chain that comes along with the company XO position.

"Absolutely. Will Rod be your *battle* for the rest of the evening?"

Tara knew what my leading question meant when I said *battle*. She had heard it before. It was in reference to the battle-buddy system soldiers are indoctrinated with beginning in basic training. Safety does come in numbers, and it was strongly encouraged to have a battle buddy (usually of the same gender, but not necessarily) when walking around base late at night.

"Yes, ma'am. Can you join us? It would be a good break."

Tara also tried to look out for me too.

"I can't tonight. I'm still waiting on a few of the team's daily reports from Schmitty. Have fun, and I'll see you in the morning."

Personnel safety was always on my mind, in one way or another. Whether I was making a call on the risk assessment for an operation my soldiers would perform in eastern Afghanistan, or giving a mandatory out-brief to soldiers who were heading home on leave—thinking about their safety was what kept me up at night and something I always harped on. Don't get me wrong, I did not live in fear over this; none of us would have been in the right job if fear dictated our actions. The very nature of the job does not attract risk-averse people. And being a leader in this environment (which transcends) means you must delegate, you must let go, and be uncomfortable; decisions must be made without you. Being a soldier, however, does not mean you are a reckless risk seeker, either.

Nonetheless, safety was always on my mind because I am a woman.

If you allow it, life can sharpen your ability to calculate danger and identify the appropriate measures that must be taken. I think back and cringe now, knowing the unnecessary risks I took in college, when I would gallop along running trails at dusk through Washington DC or thoughtlessly explore foreign cities by myself. Being aware of your surroundings is often a life skill that most people do not fully understand or develop. Nonetheless, awareness of one's personal safety is necessary wherever you go in life. Being a commander on the front lines, however, only expedited that learning curve and awareness—in more ways than I anticipated.

I started early with my company, fostering an environment of discipline and cultivating that code of acceptable behavior (remember the long-lost duffel bags—we must take care of each other), and a positive command climate. The commander does set the tone, as you learn in the military. And in the military, it is made clear that there is zero tolerance for a handful of infractions—and sexual assault was at the top of the list for absolutely no lenience. Nonetheless, it didn't necessarily matter how I felt about it or how I would objectively handle it. I was simply the first link in a chain.

The overwhelming mistrust of how the military deals with sexual assault cases is in the system.[67]

I don't believe I will disabuse anyone of the fact that there are bad apples in the honorable bunch of service members who take an oath to protect and defend. The military is no different from any other organization that tries to create unity through common ethos, but can never be 100 percent successful in this endeavor. Nevertheless, throughout my time in uniform, I felt that unity and observed military virtues in those who served alongside me. I fortunately never experienced the fear (or act) of sexual assault from one of my comrades, nor did I have to take punitive action while I was a commander. Yet we know that is not always the case.

Further, there was more to the equation when you were deployed. On any given day in Iraq or Afghanistan, it seemed like you saw just as many contractors, government employees, foreign nationals, or local workers—all of whom were people that you knew immediately had not taken the same oath that you did, were not molded to have the same ethos, or might not have been vetted or held accountable to the same degree that service members were (or should be). Add the possibility of what might happen to you if you were taken captive while on a mission, and there was plenty to be concerned about while deployed to combat. This concern never fully abated, either, since there was always some kind of salacious rumor that would stoke the fire and psyche.

Only a few days into our deployment to Afghanistan, I was able to use one of those rumors to propagate my message on personal safety—for all of my soldiers. During one of those mandatory briefings we received upon arrival to Afghanistan, I overheard a small group of soldiers whispering about how a male officer running the perimeter at Bagram was accosted by a group of local nationals and raped. Later on in the day, I overheard another group of soldiers at lunch, talking about how a female sergeant who was walking to the showers late at night was sexually assaulted by a contractor. What is often true about military RUMINT is that the story slightly changes after every exchange. Moreover, what *can* also be true is any aspect to the story. I mentioned these stories to my team leaders and told them to get the word out—and make sure that the consistent point was that every soldier needed to take personal safety seriously, at all times, and to be aware of when they might be most vulnerable. And that we needed to take care of each other.

Rules were established that soldiers were to never leave their weapons unattended, meaning out of sight or unsecured (a secured weapon would be locked up). Therefore, soldiers were more likely caught without their weapons at the gym, running the perimeter, or showering. These activities do not allow soldiers to properly wear their weapons and maintain weapon safety, so they are typically locked up and are normally the only times a soldier is without them. Thus these are times when the soldier should especially adhere to the battle-buddy system. However, the battle-buddy system did not always work, as there were not enough soldiers to go around; two personnel did not always man a shift, or teams would often have only one female on them.

I found myself in this situation countless times. My day often ended in the middle of the night, and if I did not have another female to pair up with to go to the showers, I was not going to wake up my poor lieutenant (Tara) and drag her along. Nor was

I going to skip a shower—not after spending a day in that sandy armpit of a place.

Instead, when I would finally make it to my CHU in those still, early morning hours, I would first make sure Tara was tucked safely in her bunk. I could do this without interrupting her sleep because our rooms were next to each other, separated by a thin piece of plywood that did not extend all the way to the top of the building. So I would step onto my sturdy army tough box, and peep through the opening to make sure I saw her in her sleeping bag.

Then I would grab my turquoise towel, my shower bag with pink loofah dangling from the hook by a carabineer, and my loaded weapon. I would quietly step outside and walk the hundred meters to the connex that had been converted to showers. Once there, I would find the stall at the back, which allowed the best line of sight to the doorway. I would hang my holstered pistol on the hook where my towel should have hung freely, but instead, concealed my weapon. I would then shower with the curtain open, so that I could maintain sight and reach of my Beretta, and the door.

This way, I never showered alone.

JOURNAL ENTRY FOR 28 OCTOBER 2009

"Clowns to the left of me, jokers to the right . . ."

Again, not much left in me tonight after working a seventeen-hour day. It makes perfect sense to someone to send soldiers to war with acute fatigue, perhaps so we might be greased up and ready for the ongoing fatigue intrinsic to the job? Today, the first chalk (the one I arrived with) did initial training, such as counter-IED and tons of briefings. The other two chalks arrived and settled in. I got my first look at Bagram [BAF, Bagram Airfield] in the daylight. Connexes are everywhere, and they have been converted into just about anything from arms rooms, latrines, showers, and offices. Barbed wire is a staple thorn around our perimeter, even on top of fifteen-foot tall HESCO walls.

There are more than 5,000 foreign nationals who work on BAF, and for every uniform, there is probably a civilian contractor (military-industrial complex, huh, Ike?), or an OGA (individual who works for an Other Government Agency, a pseudonym for the alphabet soup of CIA, FBI, NSA, DIA, and so on). Not to mention the presence of our coalition partners. A few of my teams will be on French and Kiwi bases—I'm looking forward to working with them. In all, I'm stuck in the middle with my soldiers.

RUMINT has already taken off, but I plan to use one of the stories I overheard today to emphasize personal safety. And, as it should be, someone has taken time to name the areas, buildings, and roads of this obnoxiously large base after too many of our fallen heroes. The main artery that parallels the airstrip is named "Disney," which is the last name of a soldier. So, no, we didn't show up in this Third World to propagate our culture (someone actually asked that in reference to the name of the road). I will never hear the word *Disney* again and not be reminded of the American soldier of the same name who lost his life fighting in Afghanistan. Reality was presented again—through several classified briefs—that we are definitely not in Kansas. I will say my prayers now, and try to get some rest.

JOURNAL ENTRY FOR 02 NOVEMBER 2009

"Where's Waldo?"

I know I will look back on tonight and shake my head that we had to "practice" a no-notice 100 percent accountability alert over here. Well, we succeeded in accounting for all our personnel and sensitive items . . . eventually. It took an additional two hours to find my wandering, real-life "Where's Waldo." This guy is a senior NCO with nearly twenty years under his belt, yet he did not tell anyone where he was on his free time. It only takes one, and there's always one. God help me when I become a parent and my child blows his curfew one day! Starkey came up with a great idea to post white boards on their CHU doors to help track where they are in their free time. Great idea! I need to make sure to tell my other team leaders to find a similar system that will work for them.

I received a fire hose of information today on current operations, while also making the rounds to do some face time with the players (mostly maneuver elements who own the area of operation [AO], and those along the intelligence side of the machine). There are a lot of names and players. De-conflicting will be a big part of my job, as will selling what my guys can do for them as collectors.

On a brighter note, I finally got through on the phone tonight and spoke a few minutes with Charles. His voice sounded so good, I didn't want to talk—just listen to him. If I think about it for too long, I will start wandering too. Your mind can be unaccounted for over here if you do not find buckets for all this. Groff's team performs their first mission tomorrow, and my other teams are set to fly out to their FOBs. It's going to be a busy day.

JOURNAL ENTRY FOR 23 JANUARY 2010

"Watch your back"

How do I even begin to write about a day like today? It pretty much started, and ended, with a call from Matt. First thing this morning, he called me after our BUB and told me two of my guys were on a convoy in a different AO! They were two of my S-6 soldiers, on a COMSEC (Communications Security) mission, sent on a convoy in Tangi Valley (where we lost Coffland). Half way through this debacle, we learned the convoy they are on is in a TIC (troops in contact). Several of them, as it turned out. Yeah, that's how I started my day.

The guys finally made it back to base. Next, my SIGINT [signal intelligence] team popped into my CP to tell me that a CH-47 had a hard landing, and when they went out to recover the bird, just thirteen miles off BAF, I sat back thinking—glad my two soldiers from HCT 21 were taking a UH-60 [utility helicopter] today. Well, it ended up being *their* mission. They were on the second '47 that landed after the first hit its front rotors against the mountainside. My girls, Carly and Ashley, were okay. After some pacing and constant checking with Task Force Gladius [in charge of this area], I was more than happy to see them when they returned to base. And this all happened by noon!

Later in the day, Mr. McKenna (contractor) stopped by and told me he is going to remove one of his defense contractors (analysts) from his contract and send him home. He said, "Sorry, I planned on relieving him a while back, but when he threatened you the other day, I knew he should not be here." I was pissed. If he already knew the guy wasn't stable, wasn't right, why in the hell did he ignore the signs? Then, with a solemn face, he sad to me, "Watch your back."

WTF? I think I may have even replied to him in that manner, and he said, "Well, I have a sick, gut feeling. He may have it out for you because you identified his misstep with our operating policy, and it was you who brought it to my attention." Great. This is not a good feeling, to fear for my physical safety (inside the wire—and *not* rocket attacks) and sense this contractor may try to retaliate, let alone disparage my name until he leaves. He's apparently already coined the derogative reference to my unit as Estrogen Battalion because there are so many women in leadership positions. On my last call to Matt tonight, he helped me file the complaint and encouraged me to talk with the BC first thing in the morning.

I regret sharing this concern with Charles when I spoke with him on the phone earlier tonight. I needed to unload and I knew he'd know what I should do . . . but he was so upset. I still don't know how much I should be telling him about the hell I am living. I wonder what he'll think when he finally does read this journal. Charles, please hold on. This too shall pass. Oh, how I look forward to putting this behind me. Well, at the very least, I look forward to that crazy man being sent back to the States and no longer posing a threat to me in Afghanistan. Isn't it ironic? I'll be safer here—in a combat zone—once he ships out. Tonight, I thank you, God, for keeping my soldiers safe. And if there's a little bit left over, can you send an angel my way too . . . for at least a few days?

During one of the first battle update briefs I attended in Afghanistan, a wise, brusque colonel called out a briefer to "give him the dirt." He yelled, "A dime dropped is a dime well spent." This means hold each other accountable, without remorse.

With equal fervor, look out for those around you too.

Be conscious of our imperfect world.[68]

★ ★ ★

Easier to Ask Forgiveness Than Permission

"Ma'am, you're going to love the Kiwis. They remind me of Texans, just with an accent."

I was thinking "sexy accent" in my head, but thought better of describing our coalition partners this way in a company BUB (battle update brief) to the colonel and operations staff. Besides, I was her only company commander who had several teams operating in provinces run by coalition partners. This was all the more reason to maintain a higher level of gravity, since there were naturally more unknowns when our troops were living, eating, enduring rocket attacks, going on missions and convoys in kinetic areas with French and New Zealanders—not Americans. A level of trust needed to be developed quickly, which was another reason I likened "them" to "us."

As I knew it would, *Texas* caught the colonel's ear and quickly translated for her. She looked up from the reports in her hand, and smiled.

"Tell me more."

"Well, ma'am, they are proud, determined, and say it like it is. Of course, we love that. We are a Texas battalion who speaks that language, so I'm confident we'll have a good bond with the Kiwis in Bamyan."

I went on to tell her about my initial assessment, which included how the Bamyan province was the only one in the country with a female governor, that the region had a higher probability for cold, winter weather over the next few months, to the unique opportunities to connect with community leaders through the Women's Center and local orphanage.

After reviewing my team reports, and sitting a few quiet moments to process, she looked at me and said, "Good assessment. Figure out how to make these missions happen, and keep me posted."

Walking out of that brief, I thought, can't things be a little easier? I'm a soldier in the United States Army, and in eight years of military service no one has taught me how to plan a humanitarian mission to an orphanage. I wish my friend Deb from the State Department was still over here so I could lean on her. Before I could even begin to think how to figure that out, Sergeant Joshua Eldridge grabbed me with his eyes from across the room, and gave me a look that said, "Let's talk." I waited for others to file out before me.

"Ma'am, I've got an idea," Josh said.

I smiled with relief since I thought he was going to tell me I had made a mistake during my update to the colonel. Josh was an incredible operations sergeant, managing the dozens of interpreters who worked alongside our soldiers, for instance, so I had thought I missed something and he was looking out for me (as he did and as good NCOs do). Also, Josh was Dr. Eldridge in his day job, a chiropractor by trade who loved being in the reserves to help squelch his fierce passion for service—recall he didn't have to deploy once the stop-loss policy ended, but he did.

I said to him, "Keep going . . ."

"Well, after hearing about the orphanage in Bamyan, I want to reach out to my church back home and see if they'll do a drive and send us cold-weather items for the children: jackets, gloves, and hats. What do you think?"

That would be awesome, but I thought to myself, can we do that? How's that going to play out if a whole bunch of (American) Christians send stuff to children in a state where Islam is the official religion? Last thing we needed was an international incident that falsely headlined, "American troops trying to convert Afghan children." Should I try to go through a non-governmental agency first, though God only knows how long that would take to coordinate?

Then, the same spirit that drove Josh to think of the idea caught up with me: we are soldiers, and this is what we do—we take initiative, we are resourceful and compassionate. We make it happen.

"Yes. Let's do it. Keep it quiet for now, and just get your church to start shipping us stuff. I'll figure out how to make this work."

Josh was beaming. He replied, "Got it! I'm on it."

Thankfully, Mike (Major Mike Crowe) was passing through BAF in a few days and I could feel out what he thought of this idea. A handful of groundhog days passed before we were sitting face-to-face in a BAF chow hall. As I suspected, Mike told me that probably the only thing the Kiwi commander hates more than being told American soldiers have to be stationed on his bases is having US brass parade through the orphanage in his battle space (I guess a lot of units have done this in the past). His candor was refreshing.

I then asked, "What if members of my team were to deliver items as a sincere act of goodwill and trust building with the local community leaders—and we kept it quiet? Who at Kiwi Base normally facilitates that?"

I followed with, "Mike, you know as well as I do that intel is about building relationships, and my team is new to the area and needs to do this."

His mischievous smile was on to me, and I could tell he was interested. He said, "Well, the chaplain, Padre Ryan, is the person who does the coordination, but of course, your mission must be approved and go through the normal chain." And, of course, what this response sounded like to me was, *talk to the padre and know forgiveness is going to be much easier than permission on this mission.*

"Hell, Mike, once all that cold weather gear for those kids shows up on a pallet, it's going to feel outright criminal to not to pass it along to those in need, right?" I said with a smile.

Mike laughed out loud. We were finishing up our lunch and he was eating the last bit of what looked like banana bread.

I asked, "Is that any good?"

He looked at me as if this question was the most outrageous thing I had asked of him today. "Of course, it's banana bread. My favorite, on my birthday, nonetheless." Now, I couldn't tell if he was kidding me about his birthday, but he was surely not joking about liking that banana bread.

I couldn't get back to my command post fast enough. I wanted to call Josh and tell him we were moving forward. And true to his word, and in a few short weeks, his entire congregation rallied and sent box after box of warm clothes and toys for the Bamyan children. The mailroom gossip travels fast, as I learned when my husband had shipped the only live Douglas fir on BAF at Christmastime, so people started asking if there was going to be a mission to the orphanage. Also, no one seemed to mind or be concerned that all this aid was coming from a church back home. Instead, everyone wanted to be on the mission that I had not exactly had approved by the Kiwis.

However, we had linked up with the padre, who was happy to introduce my team to the orphanage director sometime in February. The "sort of" approved mission was happening as a meet-and-greet, and a date was set for February 19. Special Agent Bennett advised that this needed to be kept small since there were warranted safety concerns of a large group traveling from BAF for this mission. That meant, it was just me and Josh on the bumpy STOL (short takeoff and landing) flight to Bamyan the day before. A turbulent flight had no chance of unnerving or stopping either of us, as we had both also just been through unforgettable rocket attacks a few days earlier: On Valentine's Day, while I was wrapping up a visit in Kapisa Province, I woke to the sound of IDF and mortars. That same night, rockets landed next to Josh's CHU on BAF, and he surely would not have survived if indeed the rocket had not detonated six feet underground. We were on our way.

Billy Rhodes' welcoming smile set the tone when he greeted us at the snow-covered dirt airstrip. I went right into a meeting with Mike, during which he reminded me his commander was still not in love with Americans and wanted my guys out of the AO. I then sat with the commander's chief of staff and argued for HCT 23 to stay at COP [combat outpost] Romero. Mike had given me the heads-up, so I was prepared to argue how my team had produced seventy-five reports since their arrival, far surpassing the team we'd replaced, which had a total of nineteen pathetic reports over a ten-month time span. Plus, my team had recovered weapons (RPGs, grenades, fuses, and so forth) and produced several spot reports. The COS was grumpy and sang the "one more month" song.

I just needed one more night, though, because the next day we were set to travel to the orphanage. And just as I suspected, for a day that had no trail leading up to it on how to get there, it was unforgettable. Because it not only shined a light on what's happened in Afghanistan—to the most vulnerable—it also demonstrated that people who serve have some of the very best hearts.

JOURNAL ENTRY FOR 31 DECEMBER 2009

"Kiwi Base"

My first battlefield rotation to Bamyan Province, which is solely run and operated by the New Zealand (Kiwi) military. I have one of my OMT [operational management team] stud analysts traveling with me, PFC Alex Chesna. In fact, we are coming off of a high, since last night she put the pieces of the puzzle together and helped coordinate for the recovery of stolen government equipment (as in, Humvee batteries that could be used for IEDs). She is young, wicked smart, and so pleasant to be around. I'm proud of her and hope she understands the significance of her work, and perhaps getting her out to a FOB will help her realize how critical she is to the entire intelligence cycle. Chesna and I have something in common too. We both have immediate access to all the activity for all of our teams. I wonder if she is also thinking about HCT [human intelligence collection team] 19 right now, which is hot on the trails and working every minute to identify the location of the two French journalists who were kidnapped.

There is always one more thing to pray about over here.

After a warm welcome from the teams, we grabbed some delicious food at the Kiwi chow hall. It was then that I could sit and relax for a minute, enjoy the broad smile and deep laugh of Billy Rhodes, and the great conversation with my bright young soldier Rudy Ortiz. Here's an unexpected surprise: Rudy says that having dark skin has actually been a conversation starter with the local population because they have not been exposed to diversity in this rural area. Whatever gets people talking, right?

One of the most rewarding aspects to intelligence is not just thoroughly understanding the differences, but unearthing and leveraging what we have in common. Relationship building. That's what I'll spend a good amount of time doing tomorrow when I sit with my Kiwi counterparts. For now, I'm going to go find a (momentary) hot shower to rinse the sore muscles on this tired body. This afternoon we walked up Rosie's Ridge, a good-size hill outside the backside of the FOB (elevation 9,500), which still has Soviet fighting positions dug out. Talk about history repeating itself.

JOURNAL ENTRY FOR 01 JANUARY 2010

"We can not kill our way out of this war..."

I have made sure to spend the holidays on different FOBs with different teams since I've been deployed. And it has been wonderful to begin a new year with my two Bamyan teams. The day started repairing (they don't exactly want us in their AO) and building relationships with the Kiwis. I sense I have an ally in their equivalent of an S-2, Major Mike Crowe. He's calm, sharp, and rugged handsome (I wish I could package him up and send him to my older, single sister).

After that, a mission brief before our area familiarization trip, and then we piled into two up-armored Toyota Hiluxes. We ate kebabs for lunch at Mama Najaf's in the local bazaar, and drove along the old silk trade road, the area along-side the mountains with gaping holes where the stone

Buddhas [of Bamyan] used to be carved into them (sixth-century monks did this, and the Taliban destroyed them in 2001). The mountainsides where they once were are still striking, and the caves where the monks used to live have a hollow peaceful presence—until you see that children and their families are living in them due to the extreme poverty. We passed a women's center and orphanage, and noted these would be great places to establish rapport with community leaders.

Overall, I've been surprised how much this place has moved me, and I have a strong feeling to stay. Maybe it's because the presence of the lost Buddhas that have tugged at this heart of mine—if it is still in my chest. More strange than seeing those Soviet fighting positions yesterday was seeing broken-down Soviet equipment that was just left behind, left in place, with trees and shrubs now growing around them (like, tanks!). History lessons scream that force alone does not work here . . . I wonder if my friend Deb, from Denver, felt the same way when she was here. We missed each other by a few months—she recently had a State Department assignment that had her in this village, with these beautiful Hazaran people. What a small, complicated world.

JOURNAL ENTRY FOR 19 FEBRUARY 2010

"Gain the initiative, shift the momentum"

Slept in, enjoyed a delicious smoko Kiwi breakfast with the team and left for a two-hour trip to the bazaar. Purchased beautiful pashminas, enjoyed being with the Hazaran people, and experienced life outside the FOB and felt closer to their world. Billy drove us to the Bamyan Hotel, where we went to the rooftop for an excellent view. Then back to Kiwi Base, to load up our two trucks with all the humanitarian aid.

The Kiwi chaplain, Padre Ryan, was our host and had arranged for the visit with the man who ran the orphanage. There were more than sixty orphans, and the director was gracious enough to allow us to visit their compound, share tea, laugh with the children, and pass out the toys, hats, scarfs, and more. I hugged these heavenly angels, all with yearning eyes and thirsty hearts. Their faces and small little hands, with mismatched shoes—it has all left an imprint on my heart. We stayed as long as we could, without imposing. It was difficult to leave.

Josh was beautiful to watch—you could feel the compassion emanating from him. His initiative connected the kindness of those back home to those in need over here. God, thank you for this day, and every single one of these moments. Please bless these dear children, and keep them safe.

I met with Mike Crowe at the end of this packed day to discuss the "difference" in information we are reporting so that the teams can close that gap. Mike is easy to connect with because we share a deep passion for intel. He caught me off guard when he started by saying, "Didn't *you* score a win yesterday with the COS!" His broad smile then hinted, "Come on, how did you do that?" He mentioned that the commander might change his mind on removing our team because of the conversation. I was excited to hear that. It's about relationships. And knowing the little things about another person—like this man loves banana bread. When I return to BAF, I will send him a box full of it as a thank-you, and as an apology for not fully disclosing that the mission today was a bit more than a meet-and-greet.

That makes me realize what you lose and what you gain from being over here. I know more about my soldiers and have a deeper level of understanding of those around me than I do of my family and friends back home. And that is bittersweet. For instance, I received a nice Valentine box from Charles as I was leaving, which had a stamp with my name and position (a thoughtful gesture and show of support)—an AC/DC CD and some candy.

As I dug through the rest of the box, I grew sad because the remaining items were things that were not *me*. And that's because we've had so much time apart with all these deployments, he doesn't know so many of the little things, like I prefer vegetable soup over stew, or documentaries instead of TV shows. All of these additional items were kind—he meant well and has a golden heart. It's just the deeper story to it. Moreover: if he doesn't know the little things about me, I don't know those about him. And I hate feeling so disconnected, so far away.

Last note for the day . . . We stopped by the Buddhas on our way back to Kiwi Base, climbing through the caves where the monks used to live and pray. I gathered feathers, which I plan on using for the arrows depicted on our Company Team Longbow board. Mike also gave me a Kiwi patch for my company board—and now I have a patch to represent every element my soldiers supported and worked with while over here this year. If only those feathers or those patches had an audio button to share the stories hidden in them.

JOURNAL ENTRY FOR 18 MAY 2010

"Beatings will last until morale improves"

If it's not one thing, it's another. This morning, Rudy Ortiz woke up with excruciating pain and difficulty breathing. His symptoms suggested he had a collapsed lung. Although he was stable, the request was placed to medevac him to BAF immediately (from COP Romero in Bamyan) for further tests. Just as I received an update on this, we learned that one of the convoys in Kabul near Camp Julien and the King's Palace was struck by a horrific VBIED [vehicle-borne IED]. I was in Kabul, in that area and on that convoy in April, and knew instantly the numbers were going to be high. They are always large movements of troops. First reports said more than twenty coalition forces and civilians were KIA, with more than a dozen wounded. Therefore, all medevac flights were rerouted to Kabul—all day.

What that meant for Ortiz was eventually being picked up and flown to BAF tonight. By the time he made it to the BAF hospital, his lung had completely collapsed. They put a tube in and he'll be shipped to Germany in a few hours. I feel horrible because I'll miss seeing him before he leaves country because I am on FOB Kutchback right now. God is busy over here. On another note, it was great seeing Rick and Taylor as we stepped off the helicopter ring route tonight. Schmitty and Billy are with me, and Billy will stay to cover for Nick's R&R (we always need at least three soldiers here to go out with the MRAP, otherwise they'd be stuck on the base). We'll go out to the local village tomorrow, and Rick said all reports and patterns suggest we'll be in contact. It's strange to walk into that. We've got to get out into the villages though . . . it's a terrible risk assessment to weigh, day in and day out. I'll think about that in the morning before we head out when I get the last situation report.

Now I need to send a prayer to Ortiz and fall asleep thinking about the image of Billy sitting on the tailgate of a '47 (which makes me recall my own first experience in 2003, flying over Mess-opotamia). You see, when we left BAF tonight, I knew this was going to be his first flight on a helicopter so I talked with the crew and asked if he could hook up and sit on the ramp. It has the best view, which, by the way, is one of my top three sights over here (third to seeing my soldiers safe and the faces of those little children at the orphanage in Bamyan). At night when you're traveling by helicopter, the open tailgate of a '47 allows you to see the dark Afghan sky with striking mountains, a sprinkling of stars, and the dark silhouette of another helicopter flying with you. Tonight, I watched Billy sitting on the tailgate, gazing out, memorizing that sight. Here's to the French task force's Black Rock Mantra for our mission tomorrow: "without fear, without hesitation."

JOURNAL ENTRY FOR 06 AUGUST 2010

"Amazing Grace"

It is just past six in the morning, and I am trying to get a couple hours of sleep before I have to be at the battalion BUB. I have a song stuck in my head, as I lie here trying to shut down from my all-nighter, the one I just heard play a couple hours ago on bagpipes. Within a couple weeks of arriving, to within a couple weeks from leaving, here I am—at another ramp ceremony. This time, it was for a fallen Kiwi hero. With more than two hundred American service members who showed up at sunrise, I stood in the ranks of about the same number of Kiwis in total who are serving in Afghanistan. We lined the airstrip behind the ramp of a C-17, with the peach and light blue morning sky rising from the dark mountain peaks that encircle BAF.

I thought of all the Kiwis I'd worked with since I've been here, how heartbroken they must feel to lose someone. I longed to console Mike, who has already returned to New Zealand. The best I can do is send my prayers to him, and to Lieutenant O'Donnel's family. May they sense in their hearts that the turnout this morning for the ramp ceremony is indicative of how so many are touched by an act of service like his, and how we will never forget his ultimate sacrifice.

Lieutenant O'Donnel was the first Kiwi to lose his life, to die fighting in Afghanistan. And it was on the same route my guys have traveled countless times over the past year. I'll stop that thought now, because none of it makes sense when you go down that road of "why" or "what if." I'll instead put every ounce of me into focusing on the next few days as I review the final concepts of operations for all of my teams to return to BAF. I am just a handful of days away from all of my soldiers returning from the FOBs, and finally, we'll be on our way home.

"Each day, each year, not known, is never done."

Take initiative, show compassion, and think outside the box—without fear, without hesitation.

Make sure to have banana bread when you need to deliver that apology.

★ ★ ★

What Color Is Your Cape?

She still has a yellow ribbon tied to our tree in the front yard; it has been there for more than fourteen years. When I returned home from my first deployment in 2003, I remember thanking my mom then, as we hugged and cried in the driveway, just a few feet from that ribbon. I knew that was how she honored my service overseas. It was one of the many ways she supported me. I asked her the next day, while eating bacon sandwiches with her and my dad on that first morning home (looking out the living room window at that tree), "Do you want me to take down that faded ribbon now?"

By the look on her face, you would have thought I had sworn in church, or worse, told her that Reagan was a better president than Kennedy (which would have delighted my father). With a tone that only a mother can harness, she responded, "The ribbon will remain on that tree until every service member is home from fighting this war. There is another family, right now, who is desperately missing their Marjorie."

I sheepishly nodded in agreement. Later that day, we went together to buy a new, vibrant yellow ribbon, and renewed that support as we tied the replacement to the tree. And, again, in 2010, when I returned home from my second deployment, and the ribbon out front was barely hanging on, faded so badly by the sun that it almost appeared white, I asked my mom if we could hang a new yellow ribbon together, before the end of my visit.

She smiled, and said, "Of course. But we'll have to go to a fabric store and buy a roll of ribbon. Stores around here don't sell the pre-made *Support Our Troops* bows anymore."

Long after those magnetic ribbons seen on car bumpers were no longer prevalent, and even after politicians from both parties no longer wore a flag on their lapels, moms like mine were still hanging yellow ribbons on trees. Although President Obama declared an end to combat operations in Iraq on August 31, 2010, and a flag-lowering ceremony in Kabul on December 8, 2014, marked the closure of joint US and NATO headquarters for the International Security Assistance Force (ISAF), my mom refused to retire her ribbon—her colors.[69] *Not until every service member is home,* she said. And that included those who did not wear a uniform, never forgetting her heartbreaking phone call the day she reached out to me, sobbing, that journalist James Foley had been gruesomely beheaded.

Her unshakable support and unwavering loyalty to stand behind my Frontline Generation is one of her capes. Her special strength and courage are a model—and an example of the many different kinds of heroes in this world. In this case, the color of her cape is yellow. And there was an abundance of yellow capes since September 11, 2001. I not only witnessed how my Frontline Generation went from ordinary to extraordinary during my ten years of post 9/11 service, but I also observed how those supporting us, back home, did the same.

After all, not everyone could raise his or her right hand and enlist, or be embedded on convoys in Baghdad. Yet for every person who was out front, there was an unsung hero back home who supported him or her with equal fervor. Perhaps it was the family who waited anxiously at home, sacrificing holidays to painstakingly carrying their cell phones with them every place they went for fear of missing a call. Or it could have been through strangers who mailed care packages and prayed for peace. Perhaps it was by working tirelessly to engineer technology solutions that could help reduce the overall risks to those in combat—people from all walks of life stepped up. And we must remember their commitment, like USO volunteers who stood in lonely airport terminals, oftentimes at the earliest hours of the morning, in order to wish those in uniform a safe deployment or a welcome return.[70]

It seemed almost everywhere I looked, I saw a yellow cape. In fact, the ways in which our loved ones rallied was just as important as the act of service by those who were out front. Both were done in a manner that embodies character, and the personal qualities from those who found their capes back home had a powerful and life-changing impact too. My dear friend Claire from Denver, Colorado, was the epitome of this effect.

Tiger moms, attachment parents, or those mama grizzlies have nothing on Claire—she is the formidable suburban mom who juggles work, kids, after-school sports, handwritten thank-you cards, and homemade spaghetti sauce. Claire is a fiery Italian woman—you know, the kind who is five foot nothing, and equally unapologetic and compassionate when discussing her views on current events. After 9/11, it just wasn't enough for her to support multiple organizations, in which she signed up on numerous adopt-a-soldier care package lists, even offering to watch service members' pets while they were deployed. Despite having no familial attachment, Claire embraced the military like an Italian matriarch. Therefore, it was no mistake she found her way into an industry that supported the troops, and began working for a defense contractor. That was how we first met, working for the same company while I was in between reserve activations. The bond of our friendship became an open door to one of Claire's most creative acts of support.

Claire found ways to serve post 9/11, and that unrelenting volunteerism made her an extension of the Frontline Generation. One of her most inspired contributions in 2010 resulted in an unforgettable mission my company performed in Bamyan Province, Afghanistan. It was several months into my deployment when I received an email from Claire, which probably had the subject line *Beanie Baby Idea*, as she always gets straight to the point. While cleaning out her garage the prior weekend, she found a small pile of those 1990s stuffed animals that were once all the rage. Since I was always on the back of her mind (if not the front) at that time, as she said, she believes that's where the notion came to her that she should send those small stuffed animals to me. By this point in my deployment, I had shared with her several photographs of my soldiers and me on patrol, in local villages or at the orphanage, and the images of the Afghan children stuck with her. Perhaps, she thought, I could pass along the Beanie Babies to them. With that, my company would pass along the goodwill of Americans back home, and give a friendly token of our culture.

Her outside-the-box idea was perfect for my company. Claire knew my soldiers were performing full-spectrum intelligence operations, which meant on any given day they could be involved in offensive, defensive, stability, or support operations.[71] They were not only collecting effective and timely information, but were also engaged in the complex task of shaping and influencing the local populace. Thus an unorthodox mission was well within our purview.

I replied to her email immediately: "Absolutely. Send them! I'll make sure they get into the right hands." With that, I moved on and completely forgot about her idea until over a month later, when Sergeant Vasquez knocked on the door at my command post and said, "Ma'am, you have a rather large box in the mailroom, do you want them to drop it off in your office?"

Recall, my soldiers had already received a live, six-foot-tall Douglas fir over Christmas, so the mystery of this second large shipment probably had them speculating what someone else from home had shipped me. Indeed, the box was definitely too large to carry from the mailroom, and looked as if it would split open any minute. Although I recognized the return address as Claire's, I didn't anticipate a hundred-plus Beanie Babies once I sliced open the top of the box—after all, she had said that she wanted to ship me a "small pile" she had found in her garage.

Well, it occurred to Claire that if she had a small pile in her garage, others might also have these cute but unnecessary critters in their homes, and would be more than willing to send them to me too. So, naturally, she decided to put an advertisement on Craigslist, and over a period of several weeks, she opened a post box, met people at Starbucks on her lunch break, and in the Kohl's parking lot after work, and gathered more than a hundred Beanie Babies from the Denver area. She then carefully packaged them, and paid a ridiculous postage fee to send them to my APO address in Bagram, Afghanistan.

I laughed out loud when I read her note describing her effort, which was cradled at the top of the box by colorful animal shapes. Tara, the dedicated lieutenant who shared my office, saw me melt into the very human, very real girl who was stuffed inside my uniform—for just a few minutes, that is. I invited her over to my side of the CHU so she could see for herself, and share in the joy. And this commander—who was outwardly projected as an overly serious person—couldn't resist reaching her arms into the box far enough to feel like she was collectively hugging all those silly little animals. The levity was just the right dose, just what I needed on that day and at that point in my deployment, where I was surviving the grind of regular base rocket attacks or reviewing situational reports that my soldiers were constantly facing the very real threat of combat.

An act of support, an act of kindness, can be exactly what any person needs on any given day.

With a quick turnaround, I shipped the box to a team of my soldiers in Bamyan Province. Corporal Carly Anderson, a bright and enthusiastic soldier and recent college graduate from Arizona, was one of my team leaders at the time. She helped plan and execute the mission alongside Corporal Nick Corder, activated from Hawaii, another bright and stellar soldier who shined in any position. Together, they helped build rapport and relations with a local village near a key operations base, by leaving the genuine and authentic impression that Americans were in Bamyan to support the people. Carly and Nick gave dozens of children what was most likely their first (and only) stuffed animal—a Beanie Baby from Denver, Colorado.

From care packages sent to boost soldier morale to the support symbolized in those yellow ribbons, so many back home did something (when they didn't have to) to show they cared about the Frontline Generation. What must not be forgotten from their acts of service is that we all have capes—the ability to be extraordinary. Therefore, it is not whether a person has a cape, it is if he or she chooses to wear it. And how you wear it is limitless—ask my dear friend Claire about her bundle of Beanie Babies that are now in the hands of Afghan children.

JOURNAL ENTRY FOR 29 DECEMBER 2009

"Alkida's evil grasp"

Could you imagine receiving a box full of letters from some random class of fifth graders—cheering you on in your job? It never fails to be an uplifting experience to read the letters sent to us by schoolchildren back home. Today, one of those letters thanked us for "freeing the Middle East of Alkida's evil grasp." I enjoyed the deepest, longest laugh . . . First, the spelling of Al Qaeda (AQ) is too funny, but then to see how that generation is processing this war. Is that what they are being taught about why we are here? Don't get me wrong; we are dealing with AQ and the Taliban, still, today, in 2009. It is just so bizarre, as I look at my day and all that it was, and try to wrap it into the notion of *freeing the Middle East from Alkida's evil grasp.*

Today felt like it was about motivating and leading my soldiers, from mentoring SSG Hall about commissioning options to giving SSG Winston ideas on how he can encourage his staff officer (Rod). I counseled a soldier who received divorce paperwork from his wife back home, to counseling another who will be placed on a different team due to a bleak performance review at his current base. Somewhere in between I ran like hell on the treadmill for thirty minutes to help clear my head and stay focused. Today really was about focusing on my soldiers (and a few minutes of levity when reading those letters from home), so that tomorrow, we are closer to achieving that mission of, apparently, *freeing the Middle East from Alkida's evil grasp.*

Awakenings start with individual risings.
Thus all people have it in them to help, to step up,
from championing pink ribbons for breast cancer
awareness throughout the month of October, to the
contagious unity our nation experienced after the
Boston Marathon bombings in 2013.

We can find a cure, we are Boston Strong,
and all of us have a cape—we are all capable
of being heroes in some way.

Wear your cape. Inspire. Take action.

Perhaps start by simply cleaning out your garage.
Do something with that pile of Beanie Babies.

Skin in the Game

"Well, Skip, plans have changed. Did you pack a sleeping bag, by chance?" Rick asked his interpreter after returning from the mission update brief with the French commander.

"Ah, for our day mission? No," Skip replied.

"It's not just a day mission anymore. We are staying out here tonight."

This was a bigger deal than it would normally be because it was going to be below freezing that night, and Rick and Skip were embedded with a French unit on patrol near a remote valley outside of Kabul. There were no heaters, no beds—just Afghans, Taliban, and freezing temperatures.

"This is what we're going to do." Rick turned to his trusted interpreter, sensing he was surprised from the change in plans. "We need to sleep skin on skin tonight to help keep us warm, so we'll sleep back-to-back and share my poncho liner. Okay?"

"What? You've got to be kidding, right?" Skip responded with a laugh. Granted, he was always laughing. But that night, even he knew this situation was not funny. They had spent the entire day walking several miles, on high alert, and were exhausted.

"Yes, I'm just messing with you. We will have to share the poncho though." Rick was quite a jokester himself.

Skip would have done anything Rick said, not just because he respected his "boss," and his contract had him reporting directly to Rick. He respected him deeply because of his tactical proficiency and good heart. Again, this situation provided one more instance in which they had something in common. Yes, they were also both from Texas, albeit by way of other places; Rick originally from California, and Skip originally from Afghanistan. Skip was a nickname for this Afghan American who had moved to the United States when his widowed mother bravely immigrated to Texas in the 1990s. He had spent the first decade of his life near Kabul, where he was born into a Pashtun lineage. Generous and lighthearted, he prided himself that he chose to live his life with dignity every day. And his choice to volunteer as a linguist was obviously rooted in his ability to help bridge the divide and break down the language and culture barriers—yet, no money in the world could have incentivized him to put his own life on the line. He had a passion to help US troops and innocent Afghans.

Skip laughed, again, this time reassured. He knew, like everyone else, that Rick is the kind of person who would take the shirt off his back and give it to anyone in need. This wasn't the first, or last time, these two bantered back and forth, and behaved like brothers. Taylor was back at the base, and although the contingent plan was that she could send additional supplies if needed, that wasn't an option that night.

Uniforms on, back-to-back, under one poncho, these two were freezing all night.

That night in Afghanistan, others in my company were either starting a night shift, or settling down for the night, putting one more day behind them. And the distance in which they were spread out across three provinces, nearly a half dozen locations, and hundreds of miles, was symbolic to the range in diversity that existed amongst my company—and those who were on those proverbial front lines. From Skip, a defense contractor who was alongside Rick's intelligence team every minute, to my soldiers, in which no two were alike. Most don't realize that those soldiers were not all American citizens (such as Sergeant First Class Malosi Leniu) and did not fit into those neatly defined stereotypes. What we did share was skin in the game. We were all invested. Yet "we" was not defined by what people saw on the outside.

For instance, one of my soldiers who was the epitome of professional stands out in my mind as an example. And despite the fact that he had to overcome not only the stop-loss policy (he chose to extend when it was finally lifted), he also rose above another absurd policy, "Don't ask, don't tell" (DADT). The DADT policy was instituted in 1994, and for seventeen years, the contradictory piece of legislation prohibited military personnel from discriminating against or harassing homosexual or bisexual service members or applicants, yet forbid openly homosexual or bisexual people from military service. This particular soldier in my company was a profile in courage twice over, in my opinion, because he served in uniform admirably, and was described by his good attitude and hard work ethic. Not by the fact that he was gay.

Nobody cared about that. His conduct spoke for who he was. Although the Army did not afford him the respect at the time of outwardly recognizing his identity, this soldier showed those around him the true definition of respect—he treated all people with dignity. Further, his exemplary military bearing was the greatest demonstration, because it was evidence that those who are different—for whatever reason—can honorably serve in uniform. Just as the Tuskegee Airmen, brave African American pilots who served in World War II, were an example that all people are capable of service in whatever capacity they so choose to serve, I believe that the homosexual soldier(s) who served in my company (and the military) were a transformational model too. They helped advance our military by choosing to serve well in an imperfect system.

People are who they are. This is not to say we need to be in 100 percent agreement with others, but we must agree on one thing, and that is respect. We must treat others as we ourselves would want to be treated.

I never believed in the "Don't ask, don't tell" policy. In fact, I was insulted by it, even though I am a heterosexual, because it ultimately declared that service members were not capable of respecting all people and keeping their eye on the mission, on what really mattered. Oh, how we were grossly underestimated. Turning a blind eye, or kicking the can down the road for someone else to deal with it is impracticable. I witnessed soldiers who served in that environment—soldiers who you were not supposed to ask—and they would have made any American proud by their commitment to duty, honor, and country. For the most part, my generation of service members fostered an environment that what we had in common was more important—we all volunteered to serve our country in its time of need.

Further, I witnessed these "don't ask" soldiers serve overseas, in combat zones, performing their duties to the best of their capabilities. They served alongside others, who were also judged by how well they fulfilled their job. These were service members from every walk of life, gender, color, religion, or political view. They grew up on farms in the Midwest to the rough side of big cities, they were raised by *blessed hearts* in the South, and were even born in other countries but migrated to the United States to capture their own vision of the American Dream. Each person I served with in uniform had something valuable to contribute.

There were several who were not in uniform who clearly had something valuable to contribute too. Like Skip. It is no secret that the military does not adequately fund or prioritize bilingual or multiple language skills—and to cut the Defense Department a little slack, this is an American problem. Because even though English is not the official language of our great country, it is the predominant language that even first-generation migrants seek to embrace. As a nation of immigrants, second and third generations onward overwhelmingly lose that part of their lineage.

Fortunately, there were several first- and second-generation Americans who still spoke Arabic, Kurdish, Pashtu, and Dari, who raised their right hand by volunteering to take a job like this post 9/11. Men and women not in uniform wanted to help fight this global war on terror and support their new country—they served for patriotic reasons too. At great risk to themselves, defenseless in the sense that they were not carrying any type of weapon in a combat zone (whereas, most of my soldiers had both a pistol and rifle), these people stepped up, and stepped into the fight.

I observed dozens of these interpreters who were assigned to work with our battalion while we were deployed to Afghanistan. They did so bravely and with honor, right beside US service members. I will be hard-pressed to forget Rashid, who was alongside Ashley on her mission that unearthed one of the largest weapon caches near Bagram in 2010. Or Skip, who saved countless lives by interpreting interrogations that had critical intelligence on locations of IEDs and suicide bombers.

And yes, it is correct to assume that several of these interpreters who found a way to help were also Muslim.

From the inside out, from the bottom up, people who have served in combat know what matters. That attitude prevails and ultimately permeates change. The military is one example of service, albeit a beautiful paradox; it is a hierarchical system that falls back on common sense and equality more often than not. It was the military, after all, that bucked segregation before greater parts of our society did, and it was the military that began to unlatch the turret roofs for all genders before that glass ceiling back home accumulated millions of cracks.

The military needs people from every walk of life to continue to enlist, to ensure the force is representative of our nation.[72] This is imperative because people act differently when they have to take a risk and are invested in achieving an outcome. Personal responsibility and accountability change a situation. When a commitment is required, the promise made is thought through in a different way. Nevertheless, our nation has a way to go in the area of shared sacrifice, universal responsibility, and national purpose. Recall, there was only one member of the Senate—and possibly the only member of Congress—whose child helped in the fighting in Iraq in 2003.[73]

As we know today, less than 1 percent served in uniform post 9/11. Even if you were to add all the other personnel—from defense contractors to other government organizations—it does not move that needle much beyond the 1 percent. Shared responsibility is not only what is lost when so few serve together. Because people who serve, throughout every generation, capture the true potential for the best in our humanity.

My Frontline Generation was no exception.

JOURNAL ENTRY FOR 03 JUNE 2010

"Taking the oath as a US citizen in a combat zone"

This morning I attended SFC Leniu's naturalization ceremony. He is one of my best soldiers, a true example of "what right looks like," as we say in the army. He is built like a grizzly bear, yet has a warm smile and good heart. Loving photographs of his gorgeous family cover his desk. And he treats the soldiers that he is in charge of like they are his family. General Scaparrotti and Ambassador Eikenberry were the keynote speakers who presented their certificates. It was moving beyond words, to watch seventy-two soldiers, sailors, airmen, and marines become US citizens in this clamshell tent on Bagram Airstrip. They already serve our country in uniform—in a deployed environment at that. I am enormously proud to serve with them and wonder if people back home realize that they have service members protecting their freedoms that those service members wished to have before today, before they themselves became naturalized American citizens.

The Golden Rule always applies. Even in combat.

We are more alike than we are different. And thank God we are different. The world would be pretty boring otherwise, especially if we all agreed with one another. However, recall that God made all of us in His image—amongst our diversity, we all have at least an ounce of Him in us.

Be the change you wish to see by serving well in an imperfect system.

Find common ground so that we can all make it to the higher ground.

★ ★ ★

For Love of ~~Country~~ . . . My Soldiers

"All right guys, tell me a joke, or something good, to help end this day a little better."

I was sitting with Starkey and Harritt at dinner, in the same chow hall with the same food we had been eating month after month. We were all feeling a bit deflated and concerned about the news we'd learned earlier in the day. Not a surprise, Matt had let us know the mission realignment for the ROCC team was confirmed. The more than twenty soldiers led by Starkey and Harritt would be scattered throughout the battalion battle space—eastern Afghanistan—with only a handful remaining at Bagram with Company Team Longbow.

If anyone could find a silver lining, it was these two. They remained undaunted through every curve ball, from being shoved into my company just weeks before we deployed, to writing a haiku to lift my spirits one night when we had learned another team sergeant misplaced his night vision goggles.[74] As you could imagine, locating this sensitive item turned the company upside down for forty-eight hours until they were recovered. Through good, bad, and ugly, these two were unfazed. And up to that point, I had thought their most memorable story was in the wordsmithing of an annual evaluation form for a terribly underperforming soldier, who was likened to have potential to fulfill the rank of the unit's favorite nemesis.

Nevertheless, Starkey astounded me yet again with his wit and unshakable resolve.

"In fact, I do have a story to share," he said.

I sat back and knew this was going to be good.

"There were these two kids," he said. "Each was given a room—one filled with toys, the other with horseshit. After a few hours, when they were checked on, the child in the room of toys looked bored and discontent. He said he didn't want those toys and had something else in mind. Meanwhile, the other child was happily digging through the horseshit. He was stopped and asked what he was doing and he replied, 'With all this shit, there has to be a horse in here somewhere!'"

Harritt and I laughed so loud the tables next to us turned to look and see what was the raucous. Again, Starkey brilliantly espoused perpetual optimism and levity, in parable form, at that.

Once we stopped laughing, I said, "Maybe the horse in the room is that several of the Roccstars (ROCC soldiers) will go to Fig's company."

They both nodded and Harritt said, "You're right. He's an effective leader and I know he gives a shit, too—no pun intended!"

With another laugh, albeit with a tinge of defeat, we stood up and grabbed our trash from the table. As we walked out, Starkey's parting thought stuck: "Don't worry—they also know we care."

With Starkey heading to Battalion, we split ways and Harritt and I started walking toward Dragon Village. There was not much left to say; Harritt and I both thought about the signal intelligence team. Starkey's last comment rang in my ears. That's when it hit me—fighting to keep them in my company would be selfish. Considering the goal for the mission realignment, dispersing their skills throughout eastern Afghanistan in different companies made sense. It was the best course of action for mission success. That's when I knew I had to let go.

Holding on too tight to people is a quick way to assess if you've overidentified as a leader.[75] And all that does for anyone you lead is more harm than good.

As a leader, you need to be accessible, relate, be personable, and for God's sake—laugh. You can't be a hard-ass all the time, and you *can* demand high standards (perfect discipline) in a human way too.

The very human side that was tied in by all this camouflage was the gift I had already begun to think about giving the Roccstars. When I sensed this shift was inevitable, the idea came to me that a fitting way to recognize their excellent work, their team, was perhaps by giving them a symbolic token of my appreciation. I had started picking up rocks earlier that week, and thought that could hopefully show my admiration for this departing sector of my company. That's when I turned to Harritt and asked light-heartedly, "Do you know how difficult it is to find a decent rock on this base?"

He looked at me like I was crazy, a look that could only translate to, "What the hell are you talking about? There's miserable gravel, rocks, and dirt everywhere!"

I smiled at him. "I'm surprised you haven't noticed I've been stopping to pick up rocks this week, filling up these cargo pockets." I patted the side of my leg.

Harritt laughed. "All right, what's up with you picking up rocks and what are you talking about?"

I said, "Well, you know like everyone else in this army, I'm a tad more sentimental than the average person, right?"

Harritt quickly defended me. "Hey, you have to be. Besides, the troops love that you take the guidon on every mission. That's meaningful, and we get that. Is that what you're talking about? If it's not, Top already told me that you are flying a new American flag over the command post every day so you can give one to each of the soldiers in the company when we return home. That is awesome!"

"This idea I have is separate from those, and just for the Roccstars."

Harritt was an analyst to his core, with year after year stacked on top of the next doing that kind of work in a deployed location. I could sense he loved this mental maze. He looked at me with anticipation.

"Okay. Do not tell anyone. I'll tell Starkey next time I see him so you are both in the loop. I want to give a rock to every signal intelligence soldier the last time they gather as a team, before they go to the four winds in this country. I plan on writing their name and team name on these rocks. You know, to serve as a reminder of their success, their impact, and what they did as a team. Do you think that's silly?"

"Marg, I love it. It's not silly to give them rocks. You gave them skills to achieve that mission, and they will go on to achieve more now."

I could tell by his face he meant it, and I was flattered.

"You've passed along the necessary skills they've needed too."

Harritt replied, "Thank you. I'm proud that you, my commander, have not forgotten that mission success means taking care of each other too. And that started a year ago when you crawled up everyone's ass to return those duffel bags that were left at the reserve unit."

That time felt like light years from this cool spring night in Afghanistan, where my mind was wrapped around the spring offensive. As I've learned in the military time and time again, "mission first, people always." Pay attention to the people around you. A true mark of a caring leader balances mission and people. We've all heard somewhere along the way in leadership development in the military that old saying "People don't care how much you know until they know how much you care." Yes, we must be tactically and technically proficient—and a leader must care and show it.

All that hard work preparing and overpreparing, arriving before I arrived, and at times, it all came down to something outside of that effort—it came down to how much I cared about the people I served with. All that I thought I needed to do, all along, to become a great commander, to be the leader I thought I wanted to follow, it was not for nothing. Yet the final (if not first) ingredient to this leadership recipe was with me all along. I always cared. I always cared about the person to my left and to my right. That admiration was not because I liked them—oftentimes there were people that I clearly did not like. But I had the same baseline level of respect for every person. I immediately respected them deeply and unconditionally, because they chose to serve. They chose to care about something other than themselves.

And that is not exactly easy.

This becomes even more apparent toward the end of the "grind" phase—those middle months of a deployment. One night not long after the Roccstars had packed up and moved on, Mac popped his head into my office. His face told me instantly he wanted to talk. I invited him in to sit on my hideous brown-rust-floral couch. Just a few subtle chitchat sentences, then he told me that the headquarters element of my company was worn down.

"Ma'am, they're tired. They just want to go home," Mac said.

Mac had been my trusted advisor from my first day in the company, and I valued his perspective immensely. I sat there for a moment, thinking about the simplicity of his obvious statement. The thought then came to me, if I can't bring a bit of home to them—like the can of snow that I gave my proud Wisconsin Private First Class Gempler around Christmas (a gift Claire sent my way)—how do I help them keep it together? Keep their eye on the prize, as they say. I knew ignoring the gorilla would not help, either. I needed to confront this continual fatigue and exasperation. Additionally, the level of angst observed with this team was a good litmus test for the rest of the company. The larger issue to tackle was how to take action in a way that would not only help the headquarters team, but everyone.

Mac and I brainstormed. Out of that conversation it was decided that we would ask the team where they wanted to be. We put that location on a sign, with arrows, pointing in different directions, on the front door of my command post. We turned thinking of home into a way it could fuel our effort to get through the day, and not feel lost in what feels like a never-ending story, a black hole of a place in which we were. I had to meet them where they were. Just like Mac said, they were tired and just wanted to go home. Starkey popped in on the night we were making these signs and added Germany, where his beloved Anke was. Mac longed for Tennessee; Vasquez reminded everyone we were over here because of the attacks on the World Trade Center and 9/11.

What you care about can be your strength in difficult times.

My company was clearly mine. I drew strength from many sources that year, and the soldiers in my company were absolutely one of them. Love languages are many, and when you lead, you must be multilingual. From recognizing and rewarding, to quality time and gifts (like those rocks or that can of snow), communication as a leader must be all encompassing (from information flow to commitment and appreciation). Furthermore, when we open up with each other, we learn that the miles that separate us as human beings are far fewer than those that kept us from where we wanted to be when we were deployed to Afghanistan. Leadership must originate with love. There was no doubt that we absolutely loved our country. It was in combat I learned *that* began with love for those with whom I served.

After all, people are what make a country.

And getting back into our country was unnecessarily difficult in August of that year. The Roccstars had to sneak their rocks through customs, and a grumpy agent found Starkey's and removed it from his bag. (Thankfully, the rock I took home to remember that team was not found, so I mailed it to Starkey in Germany a few weeks after our return.) The battalion came together for a week of official demobilization at Ft. Bliss, Texas. If there was ever a place where you are desperately searching for a horse, it's demobilization site!

We were so close to seeing and holding the loved ones we missed, being the places we had written on those cutout arrows just weeks earlier. Then again, it was bittersweet because for all the hellos we looked forward to, there were the impending good-byes. Of course we couldn't wait to say good riddance to some, as is the case no matter what you've been through. Nevertheless, the undeniable bonds we had formed over this past year —with strangers—were very real.

JOURNAL ENTRY FOR 12 APRIL 2010

"Athena's weapon was a bow"

Of course Starkey knows this, and shared it with me on the day we had to say good-bye to the Roccstars. Company Team Longbow will not be the same without this team. Just in time, I collected enough rocks, and found the pens that would allow me to write their names. I shared dinner with the group, and afterward went to the gym with Tara to clear my head by doing my new favorite medicine ball routine. Well, tried to clear my head . . .'[76]

JOURNAL ENTRY FOR 11 MAY 2010

"Silver linings"

I'm only thirty years old and today I found my first streak of gray hair (silver, really). Craig laughed when I shared this with him on the phone tonight, after I called him to tell him his awesome guys stopped by. He reminded me he does not have a single strand, given all the years he's been to hell and back. He's the anomaly, though, because I believe today's army has attributed to a generation of twenty-year-olds with premature gray. Now, I fall in the ranks. Last year, Charles returned from his fifteen-month deployment with gray hair, and it broke my heart. And that was due to the fact that I knew the stress he had just endured did that to him. It's just a sprinkling, on the sides; it fits in unseen with his blond, until he turns his head and the light catches it just right.

Again, I hate war. And I despise the idiots who make it more stressful. There are always those bad apples everywhere you go. The army, serving in combat, is no exception. God, I am so tired. I know I need to focus on the gems, like dear Brandi who worked with Tara and arranged for me to get a new mattress today! Out of the blue, an act of kindness, she remembered my saying the one I had was disgustingly stained and had probably been here for years. In fact, that got me thinking . . . we are over here, fighting a war, one we've been engaged in for over eight years. And fighting it one year at a time! One unit cycling through, again and again, sleeping on that same stinking mattress. What are we doing? Arghh!

I just can't go there tonight. Instead, I'll think about the care packages I received from home today, and soldiers like Brandi and Tara. I will be thankful for the endless love in this terrible place. Even though it is present in silver linings. That damn hair resembles the love I put into each day here, for the soldiers in my command.

JOURNAL ENTRY FOR 28 MAY 2010

"10,000 miles or more . . ."

Matt always says, humorously, "It's fine." And our call tonight was no exception when I had to give him an update. "It's fine," is our way to laugh through the "not fine." He was a great friend and mentor tonight as I chatted with him before my mission to Kiwi Base tomorrow. Schmitty and I are heading out there, and I've got to remember to grab the guidon in the morning before I leave. So far, it's gone with me on more than a dozen missions. What I did thankfully remember was that it's Starkey's birthday while I'm on this battlefield rotation, so I stopped by the shops today and bought him some Dr. Pepper and magazines. A group of us grabbed dinner tonight at the BBQ chow hall, which was fun. I've got to remember to start looking a few days ahead on my birthday list that I have in my green book. Forgetting birthdays over here is not an option.

JOURNAL ENTRY FOR 12 JULY 2010

"How do you measure a year in your life?"

It's 525,600 minutes. It's been a year since we were activated. It all started when the battalion first came together to train at Ft. Hunter Liggett, and then Ft. Lewis. Now we've been in Afghanistan for nine months. Although people keep commenting that we are closing in on our time over here, and "almost done," I am not exactly thrilled. There is a lot of work on the demobilization side, not to mention all those inventories, my change of command, and seeing the very best parts of my company disbanded at Ft. Bliss and scatter to the winds. I already miss my soldiers (well, most of them). I will miss fighting for them, motivating, developing, and selfishly, being inspired by them.

Today I received a box of macadamia nuts from Specialist Corder, who brought them back with him from his R&R in Hawaii. It was really nice. It reminded me of the French cheese Taylor brought me from Kapisa Province, when she was passing through BAF a few months ago. Or the beer that Greenfield left me when I insisted he sleep on the couch in my office when all the temporary bunks were full (so that he wouldn't have to be in the tents on the other side of BAF, in an open bay). I guess today will be measured in nuts, or the hour with Brandi at the gym, or joking with Mac, talking with Starkey. I hate that I'll miss the hell out of this place . . . because of these people . . . and what we accomplished together.

JOURNAL ENTRY FOR 10/11 AUGUST 2010

"You run a tight ship"

My replacement said this to me today. He may not have meant it as a compliment, since I was going line by line through the property book, but I absolutely took it that way. The day started out on a high—seeing Groff, Corder, Taylor, Willis, and Billy return to BAF, safe! Company board was finished today, just in time to be showcased at the end-of-tour award ceremony in the chapel annex. I admit, I teared up a few times, and it started when Starkey, Sam, Groff, and Schmitty were awarded Bronze Stars. Several weeks ago, I drafted their citations, doing my best to capture their exceptional performance in each of their roles. I am beyond proud.

The entire ceremony was overwhelming—foremost, to see my entire company together again! And, even in elation, a pit in my stomach will probably forever remain because Brigade refused to consider the rewrites for my CI team and for others like Tes—they all received downgraded awards. What more could I have done to rightly recognize them? I know it was not for the impact awards I drafted earlier in the tour for over a dozen soldiers (for which I worked closely with our awesome personnel team: Lynnette, Leniu, Lily, and others)—I strategically shined a spotlight on the deserving soldiers who would not be in the running (due to their roles) for Bronze Stars. The handful that didn't get approved breaks my heart.

I understand the range in these honors is wide. I received my Combat Action Badge and Bronze Star today too. And I am not delirious on where I fit in. I get that others have received CABs for far more danger and "action," just as what I gave to earn a Bronze Star Medal is different from someone else. Nonetheless, I'm honored. Moreover, I will never forget looking out at my company today and seeing their faces, the plethora of corporals that I promoted, the more than half a dozen that I reenlisted while over here, from all the missions we went on together . . . My "haiku sergeant" even sought me out afterwards, and thanked me for "being in his corner," *not* up his ass, which I was all year. He snapped to attention and saluted me. I was speechless.

Talk about a year of unexpected, from allowing people to surprise you by extending them grace, to allowing my edges to be sanded down and hug on demand, without hesitation. I squeezed Flook and Dougan (two of my Roccstars), when I saw them return to BAF. They both told me they still had their rocks. Still, I can't help but think of Schmitty's observation, "I know you're not staying in after this, ma'am. There's no Santa after captain, and no way for you to top a command in combat." He is right. And I learned today that my end-of-tour officer evaluation report put me as top rated, the number-one captain in my battalion. I nearly fell off my chair. Considering all the bumps with Texas, she rated me the best. My senior rater also wrote, "Superior command performance in combat," and "number-one military intelligence commander in [his] command." This acknowledgement from my superiors felt great, but of course, I live for the respect of my soldiers. That is the true reward at the end of the day.

These moments right now feel like life in Technicolor. And I need to spend a few more minutes packing up tonight. There's no use in trying to sneak home the *mujahideen* rifle that was gifted to me by Craig's team. Oh, how I would have loved to hand that over to my dad. It's probably been in this region since 1897, so . . . no place like home. Here it will stay. Hell, I'm going to have a tough enough time figuring out where to hide my Roccstar rock since I learned today that customs will not allow those through. Seriously, if this is what I get to worry about tonight, it's a good night. Thank you, God.

★ ★ ★

Have the audacity to ~~hope~~ love. That is truly the unmistakable tide that is the staple of my Frontline Generation—at great risk, of our own accord, we served—we cared about something and someone other than ourselves.[77]

We were earnest in how we lived and loved. When you've experienced the gravity of that, it will never leave you.

"Faith, hope, and love . . . the greatest of these is love."

Don't apologize for being tough, or for having a soft side. Both are needed to lead.

Keep searching for that horse.

★ ★ ★

Like a Girl

Have you ever been discounted, disregarded, or diminished?
Unfortunately, nearly all us have experienced this terrible feeling,
and the memory of at least one instance was poignant enough
that it probably came to mind for you almost immediately. What
still comes to mind for me when I answer that question was the
unforgettable moment when I was marginalized—from a place
that felt like the top of the world.

For more than a year, even before I had deployed to Afghanistan,
I anticipated and visualized the exhilaration of returning home.
And up until I boarded the early-morning flight on an American
Airlines jet, reality was better than what I had wished: all of my
soldiers were safe and also returning home; I served them with
every ounce of my soul; and we had left a part of the world better
than how we had found it.

It was a Friday morning when my unit was released from our
demobilization site at Ft. Bliss, Texas. Over two hundred soldiers
were shuttled to the local airport and would scatter to the wind on
dozens of different commercial flights. My soldiers would travel
to Hawaii, Wisconsin, Texas, Maryland, and Germany, to name a
few corners. That morning, I was making my way to Tennessee.

We had been back in the United States for eight days, during
which only one of those days we were given a pass to go off base

for a few hours.[78] So our first steps into the airport were pretty much the first steps toward reintegration with civilian life. We were still on military orders, so we were traveling in our uniforms, with dirt from Eastern Afghanistan still embedded in the soles of our boots. And our one carry-on luggage was most likely a ratty-looking, well-used "thirty-six-hour bag," which probably looked like it had been to Afghanistan and back.

I was carrying my bag in front of me when I stepped onto the plane with the second boarding group. I had just rounded the corner and was making my way through the first class cabin when a large older man in a disheveled suit stood up from his aisle seat—bumping into my bag and me. Without eye contact, he blurted, "One second, sweetheart, I need to grab something out of the overhead."

Stunned from being knocked into—without an apology at that— I was even more perplexed by what this stranger said. Did he just call me *sweetheart*? My parents or my husband would use that word—but even they would not call me that in a public setting while I was in my military uniform. That nonchalant term of endearment reduced my status and immediately reminded me of the old Special Forces sergeant who had called me *toots* and that memorable first drill sergeant I had encountered who gave me those ridiculous three choices of the kind of woman I could be. I had served ten honorable years, part of a generation that transformed the military—only to return to a society that still had people who put me into a category I did not choose. And this all happened on a day I was returning home from a grueling tour as a commander on the front lines.

After digging through his bag, this stranger turned to look at me, and before sliding back down into his seat, he smiled then said, "I got it. Thank you, darling."

Really? Now he was calling me *darling*? This man probably did not know that the patch on my right shoulder represented time served in combat. He surely did not register the bayonet with wreath insignia above my left pocket was a Combat Action Badge, earned for active engagement or being actively engaged by the enemy. However, one would think he would render a baseline of respect from simply seeing a military uniform. Instead, he was treating me *like a girl*. Yet *like a girl* means so much more. This girl was part of the Frontline Generation who had taken an oath to defend and protect.

I stood still in that aisle, and waited for him to recognize that I was not moving. What felt like forever (yet not as long as it took to find an IED on a convoy in eastern Afghanistan), he finally looked up at me. Once we locked eyes, I said, "I am a soldier and officer in the United States Army. You can address me as captain or ma'am."

Now it was his turn to be stunned. He stared at me and blinked. I stared right back at him.

With pride, with the knowledge that through service I was the best of a class, I smiled at this stranger. I was powerful. Even though this man in first class seating did not correctly recognize me, I knew as I turned to walk down the aisle toward coach that I was the *real* 1 percent. After I sat in my seat, quietly looking out the window as our airplane took off, I began to wonder if I would have to explain myself, my service, again. The answer to this has been a resounding yes.

As time has gone by, I have been stung by the questions during job interviews when asked, "You were just on a base when deployed, right?" to the acerbic suggestion by a "progressive" colleague that I should "tone down" the fact that I was in the military because it implied I must be closed-minded and not inclusive. The passive discrimination and misconception has been brutal. It has even been perpetuated on a national scale, as I suffered one year through an entire Veteran's Day weekend of Jos. A. Bank commercials, promoting that if you bought one suit they would donate a free *men's* suit to a veteran.[79] Yeah, I get it; they are a men's clothing store. But not all veterans are men.

People back home have not understood or misunderstood how females are capable of handling the rigors of war. That's likely due to the fact that girls are told their entire lives that they should not join the military, they are not as strong, as fast, or simply, that's what boys do. But if I love my country so much, why shouldn't I serve in the military? Gender should not be a barrier for me to claim the higher status, the honor, of becoming a veteran and accepting social responsibility as a citizen. As we know, there must always be a class of citizens who defend and protect this great country.

Regrettably, though, this great country has not fully recognized and honored all of its citizens who have served in uniform. I was reminded of that recently when reading an article about the late Lowell Steward of Los Angeles, California. Steward was a decorated Tuskegee Airman, who flew 143 missions and was awarded the Distinguished Flying Cross among other awards during World War II.[80] Yet when he *returned home*, he couldn't get approved for a *home loan* because of the color of his skin. When I read this in his obituary, I felt a powerful connection to this man, because I, too, knew how it felt to return home and not be recognized. As a woman who helped integrate our military and advance peace in some of the most gender-oppressed places in the world, female veterans who have moved on to civilian lives have been overlooked, underpaid, and underemployed.[81]

However, like Steward and like many in my generation, we did something—served in uniform and in combat—when others thought our actions seemed senseless, reckless, or unwise. Stewart or other Tuskegee Airmen may have been challenged, "Why would you put your life on the line for a country that does not extend equal rights?" Just as today, daughters of an influential senator were publically advised to avoid the military because of the threat and flawed reporting structure for sexual assaults.[82] All these years later, it is obvious African Americans made an impact: they were right—they *were* part of the change. Their act of courage to serve well in an imperfect system, their fight for recognition and access paved the road for civil rights. Now, in my lifetime, an honorable, worthy man like General Colin Powell has served as the Chairman of the Joint Chiefs of Staff.

The larger point to be made is not about race or gender or fill in the blank—it's about a progression of thought in our society. What contributes to this evolution in our understanding and acceptance is often when you can "see it to believe it."[83] Our country saw that women were serving alongside men because this generation's wars put women in new roles. I am a woman who was an intelligence officer and commander, leading men and women in combat. This very notion destroys the previous perception of women in the military—it unravels it. And what should build the new view is acknowledging the truth. The truth is, women have already led in combat. Women can be leaders in service. They already have and it is okay.

In fact, it was better than okay. We were right that women not only can do it, but they can thrive. I had the pleasure of serving with these women, and was reminded by my own commander that I had set the bar too. Given to me just a few days prior to my flight home, my end-of-deployment officer evaluation listed me as the number-one-ranked military intelligence company commander in eastern Afghanistan. That was a result of sheer grit, working twice as hard, and all the other things that you have read up to this point. Like so many other women before me, we saw in our hearts what we wanted to be, and that helped pour the foundation so all could see with their eyes.

Regardless that some may have been looking at me to succeed or fail—because I am a woman—I fulfilled my mission and served well.

My generation is responsible for making unprecedented progress in creating the new perspective of women in the military. Which is why women must continue to serve in uniform, now more than ever. We have come so far. An army analogy that translates is when you drive into an ambush. Although it may seem counter-intuitive, you are taught in the military that the highest likelihood of survival when faced with an ambush is to *drive through it*. You do not stop; you do not back up, or cautiously make your way. You must stomp on the gas and push through. This is how we advance.

Furthermore, this progression of thought must occur for both genders. Both men and women must know the Frontline Generation has proven that women can do what they have been told that they can't do. Society's biases did not break our ambitions. And we will be able to measure our success in this movement when more girls say they want to join the military. When they say that they want to serve in some capacity, which surmounts conventional norms. And someone will naturally conclude, in a progressive way, that makes sense, and that is *like a girl*.

The extent of this revelation did not take place on that final day of my deployment, on that long flight to Tennessee. On that day, which was also my birthday, I was stuck in the moment of my release, all of the good-byes, and what it felt like to walk into my new home. Charles and I had bought a house the month before, when I was home on leave (R&R), and we had been dreaming of this day because it was supposed to mark the day we would slow down, be stable, and have a break from deployments. We longed to start our family.

Yet my first night home, I had never felt more alone in my entire life. Charles had been deployed to Iraq. In fact, while my plane was flying back to the States, his plane was flying in the opposite direction, toward the Middle East. Now I was the person who could not reach out and call him at any moment, I was the person with the weight of uncertainty on my heart. As I lay in our bed that night, the excruciating silence that I had yearned for when I slept alongside Bagram's airstrip only allowed for those terrible fears to slip into my mind—the concern for his safety was all I could think about.

I resolved that I could help the situation if I stuck to my bedtime routine and write my last journal entry. I had religiously poured my heart into that brown leather book every night of my deployment. However, nothing would leave my pen. I lay in bed and tried to write . . . to no avail. I could not write. Instead, I began to cry. The sacrifice of my generation, from every level of personal commitment, was overwhelming. We have given so much.

I began to flip through the pages of my journal, reading the stories of the past year and feeling comfort that I was not entirely alone—I had my company with me, in that book. In fact, they were etched on my heart. I began to grow brave with reflection. When I turned to an early entry that captured Tara's question of Josh at the beginning of our tour, when she asked him what was the first thing he would do when he got home, I laughed out loud. She had guessed he would take a bath, and when he coaxed her to think of something better, she replied, "A bubble bath?" I never thought that nearly a year later that a bubble bath would be the runner-up to being in Charles's arms. I closed my journal, got out of bed and walked into the bathroom to turn on the hot water. So it ends, like she said it would end.

JOURNAL ENTRY FOR 26 AUGUST 2010

"Can I have a flag?"

I must wake up in two hours in order to catch a bus to the airport for my flight home. I am going home. This is my last night—on orders—for this deployment. My last communal shower, last night in a barracks, my last formation earlier this evening . . . with my company. I spent much of today correcting travel vouchers so that everyone will get paid, signing evaluations, and enjoying those conversations that are only the kind that you have when you say good-bye for good. Tonight during my final formation, we handed out the American flags that were flown over my command post in Bagram. Top helped me fly a flag every day, for every single soldier.

Final signatures were added to the company board, and heartfelt salutes and hugs, handshakes, and knowing nods were interlaced in every moment of the day. When I saw my company tonight, I was able to exhale, at last. They were all here, back in America and on their way home. So many memories today, so many I know I will never forget. Texas gave me a photo of all of the command teams and a book, "Band of Sisters," in which she scribed a short note of praise on my command time in Afghanistan. She and I came a long way this year—and I learned that we both just wanted the best for those we led. Again, to focus on what we have in common helps you prevail. A particularly warm moment was seeing other soldiers admire the flags that Top and I gave to the company. Specialist L'Oreal Wynn walked up and asked if she could have one. I luckily had an extra, and thanked her for all she did this year. I told her that I wished she had been in my company. She smiled and replied, "Me too, ma'am!" Big sigh. I gave all of me to my soldiers and it really paid off. It feels so good. Thank you, God.

JOURNAL ENTRY FOR 23 SEPTEMBER 2010

"There I go, on the road again . . . "

I spoke with my dad on the phone tonight, wishing him happy birthday. And just as almost every conversation with him, he said something so simple yet so profound. When I told him that Charles would be home soon, and that I was beyond anxious because it was the final event I needed in order for my heart to fully mend, my dad didn't miss a beat. "And for your heart to move forward," he said. Yes, Dad. Exactly. I look forward to seeing him and Mom at the Yellow Ribbon reunion in October. I can't wait to introduce them to my soldiers.

I've been home for about a month, and feeling better for all the sleep, light gym, and healthy food . . . and from all the positive phone calls with family and friends. There is a din, though, I hear and feel the rumbling, the ferocious energy and focus to turn the page. And there I go. This little bit of time away from the army, this deployment, has helped me to begin to process and digest much of the life-changing experience of this past year. First, it made me invincible in that I know my unshakable belief—service. I will continue to serve in some way.

Second, there is no one like me. And it does not serve me, or anyone else, if I play small. I have been to heaven and hell and back. I have been disappointed, surprised, empowered. Through it all, I found inspiration and heroes. I found villains and cowards. I can now better define friendship, and what I want moving forward. I still think of those wild, unbelievable moments. Some will never fade as the days keep coming—that I am certain. And that's okay. On my birthday, August 27, a Friday, I completed my deployment and flew to Nashville. What should have been a triumphant homecoming was instead, the salty, stinging reality of my generation of service members: Charles was not home. He was deployed to Iraq. Albeit a short tour, he was still *not home* when I *returned home* from combat.

His coworker picked me up from the airport, and drove me to my new home, the one Charles and I walked through and made an offer on when I was on R&R. Although Charles only had three days in the house before he had to deploy, he did an incredible job at setting it up as much as he could so I would be comfortable . . . enough to at least crawl into bed. He had flowers, a card, and some food in the fridge. He is so *loving* to do all of that. I know he was upset, too, that he would not be here for me. My anger over that was not directed toward him, though. We've both done our share—but no. The army takes just as much as it gives. And, when you realize that the "give" is as profound as it is, you are humbled because the "take" is equally powerful.

So Charles and I must toast to both of our triumphs in surviving this year when he returns home from Iraq. And, last I heard from him, that ETA is just before dinnertime tomorrow. As of now, it's 2:30 in the morning and I need to let this heart sleep. Perhaps, sleep it off. One more night. When Charles is home, I can finally let go entirely. I can finally stop worrying . . . for a little while. Happy ever after, huh? Well, I know this ride is not a straight shot, like the interstate outside of Omaha where you actually see the curve of the earth over the horizon. I will fall asleep tonight knowing so much more about the curve of this world, life, myself. That brings me to my third revelation and the last I will put to pen tonight: I have found a reservoir of faith, hope, and love within me. Don't get me wrong, I still reach for and can find strength from others. Now, though, I can draw upon a deep, deep reservoir. And God is all around, a constant breeze over that water.

Be proud of your service. It can shape inclusion, incite empowerment, and instill unshakable grit.

And that can help you do the things others said you could not do.

Sometimes your service may not be immediately recognized. Yet an act of service will prevail and will perpetuate a progression of thought.

EPILOGUE

Service Is a Force that Gives us Meaning

"Was your husband in the military?"

I was leaning through the back passenger door of my Jeep, in the parking lot of my son's daycare, when I heard a man's voice ask this question. I was trying to convince a wiggly three-year-old to sit in his car seat, and stopping the negotiation with my toddler for a split second, I turned to look out the door. I did not see anyone standing by my vehicle. So I quickly shrugged it off, and secured the buckle. After situating my son with a snack, drink, and beloved stuffed bear, I scooted out of the back seat and closed the door. Turning to walk around to the driver's side, I saw a man patiently standing behind my Jeep, holding the hand of his own squirming toddler. He and his little girl had been waiting for me to finish so they could climb into their car, which was parked next to mine.

"Oops. Sorry for the wait. I didn't realize you two were back here," I said.

"That's all right." He smiled, nodding at his little girl, and said, "I understand." Only parents of toddlers can fully relate to how long it takes to get these little people into their car seats.

He then asked, again, "Was your husband in the military?"

Aha. I *did* hear someone. But why would this man ask me that question? How could he possibly know that my husband is in the military?

He quickly identified the perplexed look on my face, and followed up with, "I was just wondering because you have a Bronze Star on your license plate."

I had forgotten. Charles insisted I order the personalized license plate when I returned home from Afghanistan in the fall of 2010. "I am so incredibly proud that you were awarded the Bronze Star Medal for your time as a commander in combat," he'd said. Touched by his words, it was still against every ounce of the quiet intelligence professional I had been molded into. Not just for humility's sake, but there are increasing safety concerns that military members remain targets here at home. Besides, I argued with him, we both know that not all accommodations are created equal in the military's flawed awards system. A lot of people have received Bronze Star Medals; I had more pride for the soldiers in my company who had been awarded them.

He quickly responded, "Exactly. That star represents not only you, but also your company. You should not discount, and never be discreet about that honorable service." Since my husband is even more so the consummate, quiet professional, his insistence had surprised me and his rationale had inspired me. I reluctantly succumbed to his persistence.

Yet this stranger in the parking lot of my son's daycare was assuming the Bronze Star was my husband's medal. Realizing this, I replied, "Yes, my husband is in the military, but that Bronze Star is mine."

It was now my turn to see a perplexed look on this man's face. He uttered, "How?"

How? Did he just ask me *how?* How was it possible that I was awarded a Bronze Star Medal? I thought, he's got to be kidding, right? People pretty much have a general idea of what it means to be awarded this medal. Therefore, his question wasn't about *how* I received it. Rather, his incredulous tone was about *how did I, as a woman,* receive the medal.

I wondered, do I rattle off the technical *how* of my citation? As a commander, I performed over twenty battlefield circulations, reviewed 200 concepts of operations that resulted in almost 400 missions, which included unearthing 80 weapon caches comprised of nearly 5,000 weapons systems that were removed from the battlefield. I balanced combat assets, enabled my team leaders, which resulted in increasing reporting that led to time-sensitive discoveries on over 40 ambushes, identified the locations of over 10 confirmed IEDs, and a suicide bomb facility that recovered two vehicle-borne IEDs. Or maybe I should mention my company developed the first database that helped streamline the training request on mission-critical systems for over 75 soldiers and coalition partners, in addition to establishing Bagram's first field detention site where one of my teams performed over 20 interrogations in compliance with ISAF and OEF policies on several high-level Taliban commanders.

But this was only the top layer to *how,* and did not fully answer his question. How I received the medal was more about not accepting choices when in my gut, I knew there were better options; to ask *why not* just as much as *why;* to believe in people *and* a mission; to focus on what we have in common, leverage differences, and build coalitions; and when needed, keep a string of Christmas lights up all year. And why this is all so important is because when you find common ground, everyone can make it to the higher ground.

Boundaries will not limit us.

In that moment, I was limited from fully responding, as I saw my son getting restless in the Jeep. I carefully chose my response: "I was also in the military and was deployed twice."

He stared at me in disbelief, and asked, "You mean to Iraq? Or Afghanistan?"

Before I could at least be grateful he didn't ask about my travels to Mesopotamia or what I may have bought in shops along the Silk Road, I swiftly replied, "Yes, both."

He strangely nodded, gave an awkward smile and walked over to his car, now helping his little girl into her car seat. As I learned from my company of interrogators—it's all about asking the right questions, and that the questions you ask can show your hand. They can expose your predisposition—your biases. It made me sad to think that a father of a young girl was coming from the limited starting place of what women can achieve, of understanding what women have already done.

On my drive home, I couldn't shake that odd exchange. I thought, if people were that misinformed about a woman's role in the military over the past ten years, they were surely missing the point for how the 1 percent repeatedly deployed, or how we united under a deeper layer of diversity, or how we selflessly committed to each other and were profiles in courage. And, again, that's just the surface.

If this stranger could not fathom that I as a women was awarded a Bronze Star, leading a company that was literally the most unfamiliar group of people thrown together at the last minute. And then we became the most successful, recognized with the most Bronze Stars (from Matt, Sam, Starkey, Schmitty, and Groff). It is likely that strangers like the father at the daycare do not know the rest of the story of my Frontline Generation—they do not know Tes served four combat tours by the age of twenty-five;

that interpreters like Skip, as a first-generation Afghan American, served honorably in combat for four years alongside US forces; Leniu was not even an American citizen when he endured rocket attacks as a US Army sergeant stationed at Bagram; Mac was not obligated under military contract to redeploy and he did; people like my mom and Claire boldly wear capes of support; and that there are men like my husband who carried the torch as both a concerned family member of a soldier—and as a soldier who has served more than his share of combat deployments.

In addition to knowing these real people, our society needs to know the Frontline Generation because it is not an exclusive 1 percent club in which the odds are stacked against anyone or everyone from becoming a member. On the contrary, admission to being part of the 1 percent who served post 9/11 is for anyone who has the courage to step up and help. And what everyone has to gain by serving is that it is a precursor to becoming a great leader, that it unites, helps us solve problems, and affords us the opportunity to pioneer new frontiers.[84]

Service fortifies you with qualities that help you push through discomfort, lean in, and break boundaries.

Moreover, service has proven to better a person and a community. And our nation needs that now more than ever. We are struggling, and we can be better than the racial collisions in Ferguson, Baltimore, Chicago and Dallas. One way to beat the increasing polarization in our society is to put people together to serve in their formative years.[85] Furthermore, we can be better than the persistent threat of government shutdowns, declining rankings in education, and a national debt that seems to increase to perpetuity. There is something to be said that for the first time since World War II, the fewest percentage of veterans are represented in Congress—a mere 20 percent. And the correlation to this decline is an unprecedented increase in vitriol and divisive bickering. This is evidence to what veterans already know. [We] veterans respect the hell out of each other, and a shared history of military service usually is the only thing that trumps partisanship.[86]

Service unites. But in America today, division is pronounced.

What we've lost is clear—our character as a nation is different. Nonetheless, what we have to gain is tremendous.

Again, service unites. Service shapes inclusion.

And timing couldn't be more critical. Where we are now is a generational cycle that is on the edge of crisis. Just as World War I was the flare for the ultimate crisis of World War II, so was 9/11.[87] We have not yet prevailed through this terrible Global War on Terror. From Boston, San Bernardino and Orlando, to Paris and Brussels, the fight continues to be taken to the homeland. There are no front lines. Which is exactly why we must learn from the Frontline Generation.

Because the people you serve beside become them. And that is both in combat and at home. Therefore, without national service as a requirement, it is incumbent upon each of us to go find each other.[88] Find Groff, Vasquez, Jessica, Deb, Vineyard, and Mac. Incredible people from every walk of life are out there, serving, living with purpose and for each other. And when you find them, you will discover that you'll find yourself. You'll be better for it. Even if you don't believe, or do not realize today, that you need to.

It may not be that far-fetched to imagine that one day we can share those knowing nods when we learn *how* we both served. Not *if* we served. I believe this is possible.[89] That is due to the fact that I have witnessed the resilient undercurrent of citizen leaders who are part of the Frontline Generation, which again includes those who were not in uniform.[90] Moreover, a veteran's desire to help does not escape them once discharged; we still want to make an impact. We don't want a handout; we want to give a hand. And if we had to choose, we don't want our nation to tell us thank you, we want them to tell us that they still need us. Because service is a force that gives us meaning.[91]

Over ten years ago, I surely did not realize the gravity of this revelation. At that time, I was simply willing to take a risk and did something that was unconventional, uncomfortable, and dangerous—and exactly what I wanted to do. I became part of a generation that transformed the military—and made it better.[92] Service provided countless and priceless unmistakable benefits. And I experienced the most unexpected benefit shortly after getting out of the military, when the little boy in the backseat of my Jeep (that has a Bronze Star license plate recognizing his mother's military performance) was diagnosed with cancer. I never could have imagined what my mind, heart, and faith would need to survive that.[93]

The story about my post 9/11 generation of service members is not just about the politics or policies of our time. It is not about the good war or the bad war. It must be about the story of purpose. The story of service. And, fittingly, the National Day of Service is now September 11, in honor and tribute to those lost and, also, as a reminder of the remarkable way Americans came together. The evidence we have today is that this story of purpose ultimately helped change history, as we've seen in the lifting of un-American policies and in all positions now being accessible to all who raise their right hand. The contagious impact that the Frontline Generation can have is our legacy of service.

And it is yours for the taking.

Because regardless of who you are, the path will not always be certain or safe. We will *all* have to push through a boundary at some point in our lives. Or, out of your control, a doctor may one day utter a breathtaking word like *cancer*. Life is asymmetric warfare. Therefore, through service, become more prepared than ever. Discover what you can do when faced with adversity. Understand what the human spirit is capable of enduring and producing.

Don't wait another minute to unearth who you want to be, how you can make a difference, and how your life will count.

Find a way to serve. You'll become the leader you want to follow. Make it your responsibility to take care of others, of your community, of your country. In turn, that is taking care of yourself.

If you've already stepped up, and have been out front—Charlie Mike. Continue the mission to help however and wherever you are in life—because those around you need you. You are a sheep dog.

My son, you are well on your way to developing your character, having a meaningful life, and breaking boundaries if you heed these lessons from my Frontline Generation.

ACKNOWLEDGMENTS

Looking back, I now realize how writing these stories were a way to help me cope with the terrible year that my husband and I thought we were going to lose our son, Henk. After his diagnosis with cancer at six months, and the gut-wrenching reality that he might not make it, I recognize how my writing about the man I wanted him to be one day was a way to fight the fear that he might not live to be a man.

Reaching deep for strength to help fight his battle with cancer, I know today that I survived because of the hardening I had received from my time in uniform. And, today, the miracle and blessing is that Henk is cancer free.

Dear son, what you taught me since that time has been remarkable too. The sheer determination in your face to roll over with a little tummy full of staples just days after your surgery, will never leave me. And you did roll over. God has a special plan for you, and I am so grateful to be your mom.

Charles, you were the first person to embolden me to write this book for Henk. When you learned that I was collecting these stories for him, one night while you were deployed and weathered out from flying, you stayed up and typed the prologue. When I woke up the next morning and found it in my inbox, your simple note explaining the attachment said, "Now you have to write a book because you have a prologue." It brought me to tears. Your unconditional love and support have always made all the difference.

I would be remiss if I didn't thank my parents for a lifetime of unconditional love and support. I know some of the choices I've made for my life—like serving in the military during a time of war—have not been easy for you. I thank you for raising me to care, and for caring enough to let me go after every dream.

Over the past three years, there have been many colleagues, friends, and family members who have supported me and encouraged me to do this. There are simply no words that can accurately capture my gratitude. All of you know exactly how you helped make this dream a reality, and I want you to know that I will never forget that either. Each and every one of you can now check off from your bucket lists *help someone achieve a dream*— because you did. Thank you.

Jamie, there is always one person who stands out, and you are it. As I've learned living in Music City, it only takes one person to believe (outside of friends and family, and someone actually connected to the road you want to take). You believed in my book from day one; you changed my life by your kindness, professional guidance, and encouragement. Thank you, with all my heart.

Formalizing my writing into a book for general consumption turned into a way for me to honor those with whom I served. To every person I served with post 9/11, you made me the better parts of who I am today, as a person and as a leader. For that, I am forever grateful to you. It was absolutely that road sign in Alabama that made me realize my son should not be the only beneficiary of the lessons you taught me, that he should not be the only one to know who you are. I wanted our country to know you, so that they, too, could be inspired and moved to serve. Never forget what you have accomplished and what we did together through service. Thank you for stepping up.

Some names have been changed to protect those who are still in service, those who are exposed to the very real dangers of this war.

I had to rely on memory to reconstruct some conversations, or fill in the shorthand of tired journal entries, which were sometimes combined when supporting a chapter. Any shortcomings or errors are mine.

I apologize for all the stories that did not make the final manuscript—every veteran has a story worth sharing. My promise to those soldiers with whom I served that were not mentioned in this book, I *will* share the best of your service and what you taught me with my son.

ENDNOTES

1   During our premarital counseling several years ago, an army chaplain asked your mom and me to describe each other as a breed of dog. It turned out to be a fun way to introduce each other. Your mom is what I affectionately describe as half German shepherd, half Labrador retriever: her focus and bite are serious, but you're also about to have a lot of fun.

2   Pew Research Center, "The Military- Civilian Gap: Fewer Family Connections," 23 November 2011, www.pewsocialtrends.org/2011/11/23/the-military-civilian-gap-fewer-family-connections/ (accessed 15 June 2016).

3   Malcolm Gladwell, *David and Goliath* (Little, Brown and Company, 2013), 161.

4   St. Jude Children's Research Hospital, "Neuroblastoma," www.stjude.org/neuroblastoma (accessed 15 June 2016).

5   Seattle Children's Hospital, "Neuroblastoma," www.seattlechildrens.org/medical-conditions/cancer-tumors/neuroblastoma/ (accessed 15 June 2016). Although several factors contribute to the level of risk for this disease, we didn't really know at that point what level our baby was considered.

6   I wanted my son to understand the significance of the piece of green nylon that now resides in a wood box on my bedside stand; it is a small piece of a military parachute, kept from his father's combat jump into Afghanistan on October 19, 2001.

7   Yet as a nation, perhaps more than ever, we must continue to be vigilant in our defense and security. That is not to say that winning a war on terror was ever our objective; the realist in most of us knows that could never, fully, be achieved.

8   A recent conversation with Brandi gave me courage, after I mentioned I was writing this, when she said, "Hey, print me a copy, too, because I want my son to read it." She had no idea how much I spoke about her in the book. She simply believed in what I was doing.

9   Of course, adhering to all responsibilities one holds with a security clearance.

10 For each other, for those back home, for so many people and for so many different reasons—and for me, it was also for my children who had not yet been born.

11 Terrorists waged a war on America before 9/11, lest we forget the embassies in Africa, the *USS Cole*, and so on.

12 "Reports that say that something hasn't happened are always interesting to me, because as we know, there are known knowns; there are things we know that we know. There are known unknowns; that is to say, there are things that we now know we don't know. But there are also unknown unknowns—there are things we do not know we don't know." —United States Secretary of Defense Donald Rumsfeld

13 Patria, Pearson, Zak, Brown, Martinez, and Effron, "Inside 'Ashley's War,' Story of a Special Ops Program That Put Woman in Afghanistan Warzones," ABC News, April 21, 2015, http://abcnews.go.com/US/inside-ashleys-war-story-special-ops-program-put/story?id=30455617 (accessed 13 July 2016).

14 I wrote a journal entry for every single day I was in Afghanistan, through the two-week demobilization process at Ft. Bliss, Texas. My last entry was written the first night I slept in my own bed and I was finally home.

15 I did not think at first that I would journal every night, but it became part of my regimen, and despite sheer exhaustion, I could not go to sleep without writing about the day. I knew then that down the road, I would want my children to not only learn from how my generation served, but I wanted them to know who served—I wanted them to know my soldiers. And that could only happen through my journals, as we would surely go in different directions once we returned home.

16 You will know what songs were on my playlist, what I was reading, what captured how I was feeling on a particular day, and read quotes that my soldiers said that rang in my ears until I wrote them down.

17 When necessary, names will be concealed in order to protect an individual's privacy.

18 I learned early on the race in life is with myself and no one else.

19 I graduated from basic training as leader of the cycle.

20 When I graduated the University of Denver, I had a yellow ribbon on my mortarboard.

21 According to a 2002 *Time Magazine* poll, 70 percent of Americans thought universal service was a good idea; recent polls also indicate volunteerism and civic participation since the 1970s are near all-time highs. After 9/11, Americans were hungry to be asked to contribute, to make some kind of sacrifice, and what they mostly remember is being asked to go shopping by the president.

22 My brother Travis joined me for moral support that morning at Denny's.

23 It's been said that "the willingness with which our young people are likely to serve in any war, no matter how justified, shall be directly proportional to how they perceive veterans of earlier wars were treated and appreciated by our nation"—though it should be noted it was not our first president (http://www.mountvernon.org/digital-encyclopedia/article/spurious-quotations/). It's an apt statement nonetheless.

24 The *New York Times* crunched the numbers and found that the military bears little resemblance to the nation it protects; its members are drawn disproportionately from the working class—the affluent and the poor tend not to serve.

25 May all who are blessed with a higher education recall this line from Lieutenant General Sir William Butler of the British army: "The nation that will insist on drawing a broad line of demarcation between the fighting man and the thinking man is liable to find its fighting done by fools and its thinking done by cowards."

26 My parents have always talked about their children, in front of their children, as if we were not there and could not hear them. It can be quite comical.

27 Oren Rawls, "Patriotic Guilt," *Los Angeles Times*, 3 November 2005, articles. latimes.com/2005/nov/03/opinion/oe-rawls3 (accessed 17 June 2016).

28 This is also when it was described as liberating, not occupying, Iraq.

29 Just when it felt like it couldn't get any worse, it would. It felt like Pink Floyd's song was stuck, repeating, "So, so you think you can tell, heaven from hell?"

30 Son, ask your dad how rotors respond to wind—sometimes you must create your own lift.

31 It's who gets the last laugh, right?

32 Perhaps that is due to being raised in a large family as a middle child, or in a diverse Southern California community. I suppose I conditioned myself to this perspective early on by covering my notebooks and pegboards with quotes by Emily Dickenson "I dwell in Possibility," and George Bernard Shaw, "You see things; and you say 'Why?' But I dream things that never were; and I say 'Why not?'"

33 A reserve unit will only go to a range once, maybe twice a year. This is not enough time to develop marksmanship familiarity and proficiency.

34 The Frontline Generation had more than their fair share of this "suck." More than one family served back-to-back deployments.

35 A nineteenth-century German field marshal, Helmuth von Moltke issued directives stating his mission, rather than orders; he understood that military strategy had to consider options, since only the first action of an operation could be planned.

36 You cannot go backwards on this.

37 The first inventory was taking command, the second was splitting my property book with the rear detachment commander before I left country for Afghanistan, the third was signing for the additional theater property equipment once I arrived in Afghanistan, the fourth was signing over the theater property to my replacement, and finally, giving it all to a new commander who would take my place back in Texas two years later.

38 Yes, Niccolo, I read your book too: "It is greater to be feared than loved."

39 It is the hectic balance of new and old that helps keep unwanted old habits at bay.

40 The point was that I should look out for "Harry" if he was still a drill sergeant, since he was quite memorable, apparently.

41 If you haven't, check out the Privilege Line activity and take the walk.

42 To paraphrase Marianne Williamson, I am a child of God . . . and it did not serve me to play small.

43 Isaiah 6:8 (NIV): Then I heard the voice of the Lord saying, "Whom shall I send? And who will go for us?" And I said, "Here am I. Send me!"

44 A great article to reference on command philosophy is by Lt. Col. (retired) Harry C. Garner, "Developing an Effective Command Philosophy." Military Review. September–October 2012.

45 George E. Reed, "Toxic Leadership," *Military Review*, July–August 2004.

46 Toxic leaders are often people who want to be liked. But a mentor once told me that as a leader, if everyone likes you, you are doing something wrong. Point well taken.

47 From the US Army website, "Leadership Training," www.goarmy.com/soldier-life/being-a-soldier/ongoing-training/leadership-training.html (accessed 16 September 2014).

48 Harry C. Garner, "Developing an Effective Command Philosophy," *Military Review*, September–October 2012.

49 Tom Rath, *Strengths Finder 2.0*. It is a quick read and an eye-opening experience to understand what you are really great at.

50 This has been my longstanding philosophy, even before I knew how to describe it through the more recent works submitted by Rath.

51 Steven Pinker, "The Moral Instinct," *New York Times*, 13 January 2008. Reference to the Moral Foundations Questionnaire by Jesse Graham, Jonathan Haidt, and Brian Nosek. As one of my revered professors pointed out, it is possible for someone to intently be more ethical.

52 "The golden moments in the stream of life rush past us, and we see nothing but sand; the angels come to visit us, and we only know them when they are gone." — George Elliott

53 Linda Ellis, "The Dash," www.linda-ellis.com/the-dash-the-dash-poem-by-linda-ellis-.html (accessed 19 June 2016).

54 The ODA (operational detachment alpha) is a highly trained twelve-man Special Forces team that is deployed in rapid-response situations.

55 Secondarily, growth opportunities for the individual and organization were a welcome side effect.

56 "Women in the Army," US Army, www.army.mil/women/ (accessed 19 June 2016).

57 Darlene M. Iskra, "Women are Heroes, Too," *Time* magazine, 24 August 2011, nation.time.com/2011/08/24/women-are-heroes-too/ (accessed 19 June 2016).

58 Janet and Lynnette, you inspired me every day—and still do.

59 Read Gayle Lemmon's book, *Ashley's War* (Harper First Edition, 2015) for more information.

60 For the word anatomy, I believe one can substitute "race, religion, sexual orientation . . ."

61 Read *David and Goliath* by Malcolm Gladwell.

62 General McChrystal said it best in his autobiography, that "the calamity is to not have the force the military needs in order to accomplish the missions we will have in our future."

63 Tanya L. Domi, "Women in Combat: Policy Catches Up With Reality," *New York Times*, 8 February 2013, www.nytimes.com/2013/02/09/opinion/women-in-combat-policy-catches-up-with-reality.html?_r=0 (accessed 19 June 2016).

64 "The Combat Exclusion Policy was lifted as of January 24, 2013, following a unanimous recommendation by the Joint Chiefs of Staff. Both men and women are eligible to serve in front line combat and complete combat operations. The lifting of the ban was announced at a Pentagon press conference by Defense Secretary Leon E. Panetta, and the joint chiefs chairman, Army Gen. Martin E. Dempsey. Panetta said that the ban was lifted because 'If members of our military can meet the qualifications for a job, then they should have the right to serve, regardless of creed, color, gender or sexual orientation.' The various service branches were given until January 2016 to implement changes and submit requests to exclude specific Military Occupational Specialties from the ban being lifted. Panetta further said that initial implementation plans were to be submitted to him by May 15th, 2014." See: "Combat Exclusion Policy," Wikipedia, en.m.wikipedia.org/wiki/Combat_Exclusion_Policy; and Larry Abramson, "Women In Combat: Pbstacles Remain As Exclusion Policy Ends," NPR, 15 May 2013, www.npr.org/2013/05/15/184042652/women-in-combat-obstacles-remain-as-exclusion-policy-ends. (Both accessed 19 June 2016.)

65 Gladwell, *David and Goliath*, 161.

66 Jerry Useem wrote an excellent article in the *Atlantic* (May 2016), "Is Grit Overrated?"

67 A pilot wouldn't ask a doctor to fly his airplane, right? Sexual assaults are a terrible crime. Period. They need to be handled in a legal system. And the fear of them erodes unity cohesion. I needed to trust in the men and women in my ranks. Especially when I needed to take off my rank while on missions in Afghanistan.

68 We all need angels. Son, I wish I could keep you in a bubble and protect you from the ugly side of this world. There will always be danger, whether you are walking alone at night in a safe part of town, or patrolling eastern Afghanistan. You need to always take the necessary precautions.

69 Sarah Lazare, "NATO Symbolically Lowers Flag in Afghanistan, But US War To March On," 8 December 2014, Common Dreams, www.commondreams.org/news/2014/12/08/nato-symbolically-lowers-flag-afghanistan-us-war-march (accessed 26 August 2015); and Helene Cooper and Sheryl Gay Stolberg, "Obama Declares an End to Combat Mission in Iraq," *New York Times*, 31 August 2010, www.nytimes.com/2010/09/01/world/01military.html?pagewanted=all&_r=0 (accessed 26 August 2015).

70 See sites such as this one: the Maine Troop Greeters, www.flybangor.com/troop-greeters (accessed 26 August 2015).

71 "Intelligence in Full Spectrum Operations," © GlobalSecurity.org, www.globalsecurity.org/intell/library/policy/army/fm/2-0/chap3.htm (accessed 26 August 2015).

72 Jeremy Bender, "These 22 Charts Reveal Who Serves In America's Military," Business Insider, www.businessinsider.com/us-military-demographics-2014-8?op=1 (accessed 20 June 2016).

73 Sheryl Gay Stolberg, "A Nation at War: Children of Lawmakers; Senators' Sons in War: An Army of One," *New York Times*, 22 March 2003, www.nytimes.com/2003/03/22/us/a-nation-at-war-children-of-lawmakers-senators-sons-in-war-an-army-of-one.html (accessed 20 June 2016).

74 Snow covered connexes, a sergeant did not secure, Poof! A DAGRs gone.

75 If you haven't already, watch *Twelve O'Clock High*.

76 I didn't realize it then, although I pondered it in my journals, but I often wondered as a commander if so many of the new feelings I had were what it would feel like to be a parent—the overwhelming responsibility to care for another life. As I would discover years later when I finally had my first child, so much was the same. Albeit two distinct rites of passage—becoming a combat veteran and becoming a parent—one would probably assume they do not have an ounce in common. Yet to this day, they are the two experiences in my life in which I have witnessed friends and strangers alike rally behind me with unconditional support. Furthermore, when you serve in combat or become a parent, it is no longer about you!

77 A rising tide lifts all boats. May the legacy of service do the same.

78 No surprise, a few soldiers from A and B Companies blew off the curfew on the night of our first pass, blatantly broke General Order #1, and were picked up at a local strip club. All off-post passes were revoked for the remainder of our time at demobilization.

79 The Uniform of Success event in 2013 (buy one give one to the Gary Sinise Foundation over Veteran's Day week). When I did some research and learned it was Lt. Dan, I was confused, because he frequently went to the front lines to support us. He knew women and men were serving. I'll have to ask him about this one day when we eventually meet.

80 Scott Neuman, "Decorated Tuskegee Airman Lowell Steward Dies At 95," *The Two-Way*, 20 December 2014, NPR, www.npr.org/sections/thetwo-way/2014/12/20/372126643/decorated-tuskegee-airman-lowell-steward-dies-at-95 (accessed 26 August 2015).

81 Sandy M. Fernández, "These Women Need You!" 13 October 2014, *Redbook*, www.redbookmag.com/life/mom-kids/news/a19189/michelle-obama-veterans/ (accessed 26 August 2015).

82 "McCain Advises Women to Avoid the Military," UPI wire service, 5 June 2013, on Military.com, www.military.com/daily-news/2013/06/05/mccain-advises-women-to-avoid-the-military.html (accessed 26 August 2015).

83 *Vanderbilt Magazine*, Winter 2016, has an excellent article on ballot bias and the subconscious sexism that prevails. People can overcome unconscious tendencies.

84 Boundaries are borders, not limits.

85 More than 90 percent of post 9/11 veterans believe that giving back to the community is a basic responsibility; they are more likely than their civilian counterparts to fill leadership roles in civic organizations, and more likely to vote.

86 Christina Wood, "Campaigning on Service," *Military Officer* (MOAA), November 2015.

87 To learn more about generational cycles, check out Amy Lynch and Neil Howe.

88 I just finished Sebastian Junger's book *Tribe*, and loved it. I encourage you to pick it up.

89 "It must be laid down as a primary position, and the basis of our system, that every Citizen who enjoys the protection of a free Government, owes not only a proportion of his property, but even his personal services to the defence of it . . ." —George Washington, letter to Alexander Hamilton, 2 May 1783

90 From interpreters to dedicated family and friends who found their capes, so many different players volunteered to be out front, to be exposed, and all of those examples can be an inspiration. Their paths could add value to yours if you choose to emulate them.

91 Check out *War Is a Force that Gives Us Meaning* by Chris Hedges.

92 I didn't expect that once I left the military, I would face a similar battle and now be required to help transform my nation to recognize and embrace the power of service.

93 The truth is, today, the best way for my son to see the example of those Frontline Generation characteristics is by my continuing to serve—the mission continues. He will never see me in a uniform besides looking through those old photographs. But he can see me live the qualities of my generation by my continuing to serve at home, in my community, in some way. And, of course, I believe most any parent wants to give his or her child the world, but more importantly, instill in them character.

ABOUT THE AUTHOR

Marjorie K. Eastman was born and raised in Southern California. She earned her bachelors degree in political science from one of the top ten-ranked programs in the country, at the University of California, San Diego. As an undergraduate, she was competitively selected as a White House intern and also studied abroad at the University College London, School for Slavonic and East European Studies. She attended the Josef Korbel School of International Studies, University of Denver, where she earned her master's degree in International Security, with concentrations in homeland security, intelligence, and human rights. During her graduate studies, she was one of fifty-six students selected nationally for the Federal Bureau of Investigation's Honors Internship Program. She also has an MBA from the Owen Graduate School of Management, Vanderbilt University.

Eastman served as a United States Army intelligence officer and commander. Her ten years of post 9/11 military service include two combat deployments, one in support of Operation Iraqi Freedom, the other in support of Operation Enduring Freedom in Afghanistan. She started out enlisted and received the rare honor of being awarded a direct commission within her first two years of service. Her final duty was to command more than one hundred soldiers in Afghanistan to successfully fulfill their mission and safely return home. She was ranked the number one military intelligence company commander in Eastern Afghanistan for the deployment cycle of 2009-2010, awarded the Bronze Star for meritorious service as a combat commander, and received the Combat Action Badge.

Eastman has been recognized by the Nashville Business Journal with the 2015 Award for Veteran Leading in Business and has been described as a veteran thought leader in PBS's Veterans Coming Home initiative. She is involved with charities and boards that support girls, women, and veterans. More recently, she has filled the role of president and COO of the YWCA Nashville & Middle Tennessee, a 118-year-old nonprofit that is on a mission to eliminate racism, empower women, and promote peace, justice, freedom, and dignity for all; as regional representative for Girls on the Run Middle Tennessee; and she helped launch the Nashville Service Platoon for The Mission Continues.

Eastman currently serves as a founding member of the Nashville Serving Veterans Community Board. She speaks regularly to a variety of corporations and organizations, and enjoys coaching young girls with a curriculum that combines training for a 5k running event and lessons that inspire them to be joyful, healthy, and confident (Crossfit Endurance Certified).

Eastman is also a spouse of a soldier, and understands the perspective from that of a military family member. She lives in Tennessee with her husband, Charles, and their son, Henk.

CPSIA information can be obtained
at www.ICGtesting.com
Printed in the USA
LVOW08s0140100817
544407LV00006B/654/P